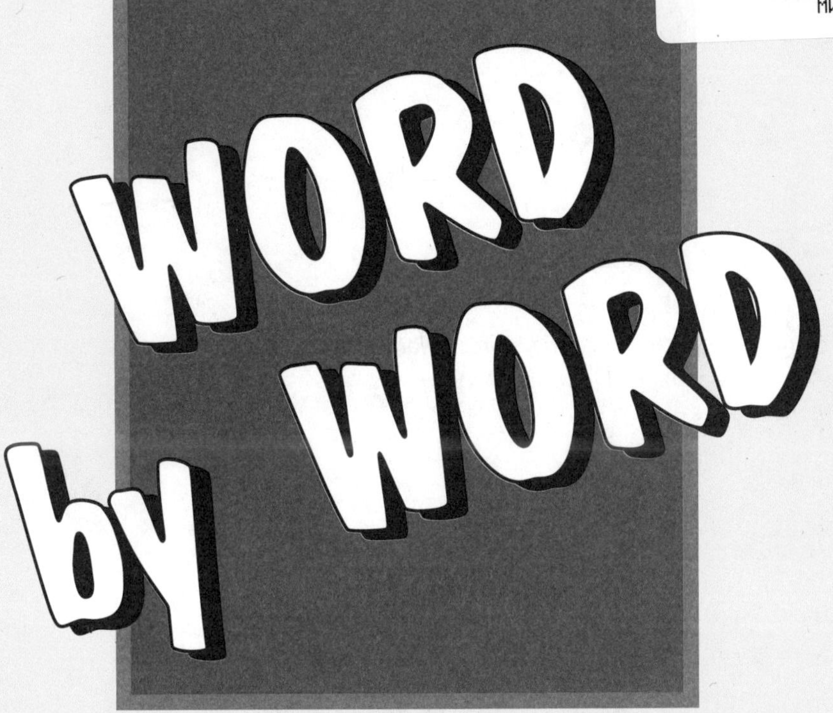

영 · 한 그림 사전

English/Korean Picture Dictionary

Steven J. Molinsky · Bill Bliss

Lee Chang-soo 이 창수
Yang Eun-sook 양 은숙

Acquisitions editor: *Tina B. Carver*
Director of Production and Manufacturing: *Aliza Greenblatt*
Electronic Production/Design Manager: *Dominick Mosco*
Production Editor: *Ken Liao*
Composition: *Graphicraft Typesetters Ltd.*
Interior design: *Kenny Beck*
Cover supervisor and cover design: *Merle Krumper*
Buyer/scheduler: *Ray Keating*

Illustrated by RICHARD E. HILL

A Pearson Education Company
Pearson Education, 10 Bank Street, White Plains, NY. 10606

Printed in the United States of America

10 9

ISBN 0-13-125840-0

목차

머리말

본 Word by Word 그림사전에는 3,000여개의 단어가 칼라 삽화와 함께 수록되어 있습니다. 본 혁신적인 그림사전에는 학생들이 여러가지 다양한 상황이나 문맥에서 효과적으로 의사소통을 하는데 필요한 필수 어휘들이 실려있습니다.

본 Word by Word는 어휘를 100 개의 주제별 단원으로 분류하여 이단원들을 학생들의 주변의 세계에서 점차 광범위한 세계로 나아가도록 배열하였습니다. 앞 단원의 가족, 가정 및 일상생활에 관한 내용들은 점차 사회, 학교, 직장, 쇼핑, 레크리에이션 그리고 다른 주제 등으로 확대됩니다. Word by Word는 일상생활에 중요한 언어능력을 폭넓게 다루고, 학과목 및 과외활동에 대한 어휘들도 다룹니다. 각 단원은 독립적으로 구성되어 있기 때문에 주어진 순서대로 사용해도 되고, 또는 임의의 순서를 정해서 사용해도 됩니다.

사용자의 편의를 위해서 Word by Word의 단원들을 목차에서는 순차적으로, 주제별 색인에서는 알파벳순으로 찾아볼 수 있도록 하였습니다. 이와 함께 부록에 실려 있는 어휘목록을 사용하면 본 그림사전에 수록되어 있는 모든 단어와 주제들을 쉽고 빠르게 찾아볼 수 있습니다.

Word by Word 그림사전은 모든 수준의 교육을 위한 다양한 인쇄 및 시청각 보조자료를 제공하는 Word by Word 어휘 향상 프로그램의 핵심입니다. 보조자료로는 3단계(기초, 초급, 중급)로 이뤄진 Workbooks, Teacher's Resource Book, Handbook of Vocabulary Teaching Strategies, Audio Program, Wall Charts, Color Transparencies, Vocabulary Game Cards, Song Album 및 Song Book. Testing Program 등이 있습니다.

본 Word by Word는 문맥 안에서 단어를 익힐 수 있도록 해줍니다. 각 페이지에 나온 모델대화들은 이 단어를 이용하여 의미있는 대화를 할 수 있는 상황들을 제시합니다. 이 모델들은 학생들이 활기차고 상호적인 대화연습에 참여하는데 기초가 됩니다. 또한, 각 단원의 쓰기 및 토론문제는 학생들로 하여금 그들의 경험, 생각, 의견 그리고 자기 자신과 그들의 문화및 국가에 관한 정보를 공유하는 과정에서 해당 어휘와 주제를 그들 자신들의 생활에 연결시킬 수 있도록 해줍니다. 이런식으로, 학생들은 "한 단어 한 단어씩" 서로를 알아가게 됩니다.

Word by Word를 사용함에 있어서, 우리는 선생님들의 지도 방법과 학생들의 필요와 능력이 조화를 이루는 접근방법들을 개발해 나갈 것을 권장합니다. 각 단원의 어휘를 소개하고 연습하는데 다음의 방법들을 함께 사용하면 도움이 될 것입니다.

1. 어휘예습: 학생들과 함께 이미 알고 있는 각 단원의 단어들을 순서없이 말하여 그것들을 칠판에 쓰거나, 학생들로 하여금 Wall Chart나 transparency 또는 Word by Word에 나온 그림을 보도록 하여 학생들이 익숙한 단어를 찾도록 함으로써 어휘에 대한 사전 지식을 활성화 한다.

2. 어휘소개: 각 단어의 그림을 가리키며 그 단어를 발음하여, 학생들로하여금 전체 또는 개별적으로 따라서 발음하도록 한다. 해당 어휘에 대한 학생들의 이해와 발음을 점검한다.

3. 어휘연습: 학생들로 하여금 학급전체, 혹은 소그룹이나 짝을 지어 어휘를 연습하도록 한다. 단어를 불러주거나, 칠판에 쓴 후 학생들로 하여금 해당 그림을 가리키거나 번호를 말하도록 한다. 또는 반대로 어떤 그림을 가리키거나 번호를 말한 후, 학생들로하여금 해당 단어를 말하도록 한다.

4. 모델대화 연습:일부 단원은 어휘목록상 첫번째 단어를 이용하여 모델대화를 제시하였고, 또 일부 단원의 모델대화에서는 단어를 삽입하여 연습할 수 있도록 빈칸 채우기식 대화의 형태로 되어있다. (빈칸 채우기식 대화의 경우, 괄호 안의 숫자들은 대화연습에 사용할 수 있는 단어를 나타낸다. 괄호 안에 번호가 없을 경우, 해당 페이지의 모든 단어들을 사용할 수 있다.)

모델대화 연습에 있어서는 다음과 같은 단계를 권장합니다.

a. 예습:학생들이 모델대화의 그림을 보고 대화자가 누구인지 그리고 그 대화가 어디에서 일어나고 있는지에 관해서 논의한다.

b. 교사가 모델대화를 제시하고, 학생들이 그 상황과 어휘들을 이해하고 있는지를 점검한다.

c. 학생들이 대화의 각 문장을 학급전체 또는 개별적으로 따라한다.

d. 학생들이 짝을 지어 모델 대화를 연습한다.

e. 두 명의 학생이 해당 모델에 기초하여, 어휘목록상의 다른 단어를 사용하여 새로운 대화를 소개한다.

f. 학생들은 짝을 지어 그 모델에 기초해 다른 단어들을 사용하여 새로운 대화를 연습한다.

g. 각 짝별로 그들이 연습한 대화를 발표한다.

5. 추가 대화연습: 대부분의 단원들에는 학습한 어휘들을 사용해서 보다 많은 대화 연습을 할 수 있도록 두 개의 빈칸 채우기식 대화가 추가로 제시되어 있다.(이 추가 대화들은 페이지 하단 노랑 바탕의 부분에 실려있다.) 학생들로 하여금 원하는 단어를 사용해서 이들 대화를 연습하고 발표하도록 한다.

6. 쓰기와 철자 연습: 학생들로 하여금 학급전체, 또는 소그룹이나 짝을 지어 단어의 철자를 연습하도록 한다. 단어를 말하거나, 철자를 불러주어 학생들로 하여금 그 단어를 받아 쓴 후, 해당 사물의 그림을 가리키거나 번호를 말하도록 한다. 또는, 어떤 사물의 그림을 지적하거나 해당 번호를 말해 학생들로 하여금 그 단어를 쓰게 한다.

7. 토론 주제, 작문, 일기, 문집: Word by Word의 각 단원에는 하나 이상의 토론 및 작문 문제가 실려있다. (이 질문들은 페이지 하단에 초록 바탕의 부분에 실려있다.) 학생들로 하여금 이 질문에 학급전체, 또는 소그룹이나 짝을 지어 대답하도록 한다. 또는, 학생들로 하여금 답을 집에서 작성하도록 하여 그것을 다른 학생들과 돌려보고, 학급전체나 소그룹별로 혹은 짝을 지어 토론하도록 한다.

학생들로 하여금 그들이 쓴 글을 일기장으로 모아가도록 한다. 시간적 여유가 있는 경우, 선생님은 각 학생들의 일기장에 학생들이 쓴 것에 대한 논평 뿐만 아니라 자신의 의견과 경험을 적어 준다. 선생님이 학생들의 작문을 모아 둔다면, 이것들은 학생들의 영어학습의 향상을 보여주는 좋은 자료가 된다.

8. 의사소통 연습: Word by Word Teacher's Resource Book은 학생들의 서로 다른 학습방법이나 특정한 능력 및 장점들을 활용하도록 고안된 게임, 문제풀이, 자유토론, 율동, 그림 그리기, 판토마임, 역할연습 및 기타 활동들로 가득하다. 각 단원마다 학생들의 흥미를 유발시킬 수 있는 새롭고 재미있는 어휘학습 강화의 수단으로 한 두 개의 이러한 활동들을 이용하도록 한다.

본 Word by Word는 학생들에게 대화를 통한 의미있고 활동적인 영어어휘 연습방법을 제시하는데 그 목표를 두고 있습니다. 본프로그램의 취지를 전달함에 있어서 다음과 같은 기본 정신도 함께 전달할 수 있길 바랍니다. 즉, 어휘를 공부하는 것도 상호적이고, 학생들의 생활과 연관되며, 학생들의 서로 다른 장점과 학습방법을 반영할 수 있으며, 재미있을 수 있다는 것입니다.

Steven J. Molinsky
Bill Bliss

The *Word by Word* Picture Dictionary presents more than 3,000 vocabulary words through lively full-color illustrations. This innovative Picture Dictionary offers students the essential vocabulary they need to communicate effectively in a wide range of relevant situations and contexts.

Word by Word organizes the vocabulary into 100 thematic units, providing a careful sequence of lessons that range from the immediate world of the student to the world at large. Early units on the family, the home, and daily activities lead to lessons on the community, school, workplace, shopping, recreation, and other topics. *Word by Word* offers extensive coverage of important lifeskill competencies and the vocabulary of school subjects and extracurricular activities. Since each unit is self-contained, *Word by Word* can be used either sequentially or in any desired order.

For users' convenience, the units in *Word by Word* are listed two ways: sequentially in the Table of Contents, and alphabetically in the Thematic Index. These resources, combined with the Glossary in the appendix, allow students and teachers to quickly and easily locate all words and topics in the Picture Dictionary.

The *Word by Word* Picture Dictionary is the centerpiece of the complete *Word by Word* Vocabulary Development Program, which offers a wide selection of print and media support materials for instruction at all levels. Ancillary materials include Workbooks at three different levels (Literacy, Beginning, and Intermediate), a Teacher's Resource Book, a Handbook of Vocabulary Teaching Strategies, a complete Audio Program, Wall Charts, Color Transparencies, Vocabulary Game Cards, a Song Album and accompanying Song Book, and a Testing Program. Bilingual editions of the Picture Dictionary are also available.

Teaching Strategies

Word by Word presents vocabulary words in context. Model conversations depict situations in which people use the words in meaningful communication. These models become the basis for students to engage in dynamic, interactive conversational practice. In addition, writing and discussion questions in each unit encourage students to relate the vocabulary and themes to their own lives as they share experiences, thoughts, opinions, and information about themselves, their cultures, and their countries. In this way, students get to know each other "word by word."

In using *Word by Word,* we encourage you to develop approaches and strategies that are compatible with your own teaching style and the needs and abilities of your students. You may find it helpful to incorporate some of the following techniques for presenting and practicing the vocabulary in each unit.

1. *Previewing the Vocabulary:* Activate students' prior knowledge of the vocabulary either by brainstorming with students the words in the unit they already know and writing them on the board, or by having students look at the Wall Chart, the transparency, or the illustration in *Word by Word* and identify the words they are familiar with.

2. *Presenting the Vocabulary:* Point to the picture of each word, say the word, and have the class repeat it chorally and individually. Check students' understanding and pronunciation of the vocabulary.

3. *Vocabulary Practice:* Have students practice the vocabulary as a class, in pairs, or in small groups. Say or write a word, and have students point to the item or tell the number. Or, point to an item or give the number, and have students say the word.

4. *Model Conversation Practice:* Some units have model conversations that use the first word in the vocabulary list. Other models

are in the form of *skeletal dialogs,* in which vocabulary words can be inserted. (In many skeletal dialogs, bracketed numbers indicate which words can be used to practice the conversation. If no bracketed numbers appear, all the words on the page can be used.)

The following steps are recommended for Model Conversation Practice:

a. Preview: Students look at the model illustration and discuss who they think the speakers are and where the conversation takes place.

b. The teacher presents the model and checks students' understanding of the situation and the vocabulary.

c. Students repeat each line of the conversation chorally or individually.

d. Students practice the model in pairs.

e. A pair of students presents a new conversation based on the model, but using a different word from the vocabulary list.

f. In pairs, students practice several new conversations based on the model, using different vocabulary words.

g. Pairs present their conversations to the class.

5. *Additional Conversation Practice:* Many units provide two additional skeletal dialogs for further conversation practice with the vocabulary. (These can be found in a yellow-shaded area at the bottom of the page.) Have students practice and present these conversations using any words they wish.

6. *Writing and Spelling Practice:* Have students practice spelling the words as a class, in pairs, or in small groups. Say or spell a word, and have students write it and then point to the picture of the item or tell the number. Or, point to a picture of an item or give the number, and have students write the word.

7. *Themes for Discussion, Composition, Journals, and Portfolios:* Each unit of *Word by Word* provides one or more questions for discussion and composition. (These can be found in a green-shaded area at the bottom of the page.) Have students respond to the questions as a class, in pairs, or in small groups. Or, have students write their responses at home, share their written work with other students, and discuss as a class, in pairs, or in small groups.

Students may enjoy keeping a journal of their written work. If time permits, you may want to write a response in each student's journal, sharing your own opinions and experiences as well as reacting to what the student has written. If you are keeping portfolios of students' work, these compositions serve as excellent examples of students' progress in learning English.

8. *Communication Activities:* The *Word by Word* Teacher's Resource Book provides a wealth of games, tasks, brainstorming, discussion, movement, drawing, miming, role-playing, and other activities designed to take advantage of students' different learning styles and particular abilities and strengths. For each unit, choose one or more of these activities to reinforce students' vocabulary learning in a way that is stimulating, creative, and enjoyable.

Word by Word aims to offer students a communicative, meaningful, and lively way of practicing English vocabulary. In conveying to you the substance of our program, we hope that we have also conveyed the spirit: that learning vocabulary can be genuinely interactive . . . relevant to our students' lives . . . responsive to students' differing strengths and learning styles . . . and fun!

Steven J. Molinsky
Bill Bliss

자기 소개

A. What's your **name**?
B. *Nancy Ann Peterson.*

APPLICATION

Name (1): Nancy (2) first — Ann (3) middle — Peterson (4) last

Address (5): 42 (6) number — Main Street (7) street — #5A (8) apt.

Long Beach, (9) city — CA (10) state — 22960 (11) zip code

Telephone: (213) (12) 684-1196 (13)

SSN: 045-61-8947 (14)

이름	**1.** name
이름	**2.** first name
중간 이름	**3.** middle name
성	**4.** last name/family name/ surname
주소	**5.** address
거리번호	**6.** street number
거리 / 가	**7.** street
아파트 번호	**8.** apartment number
시	**9.** city
주	**10.** state
우편번호	**11.** zip code
지역번호	**12.** area code
전화번호	**13.** telephone number/ phone number
사회보장번호 / 주민등록 번호	**14.** social security number

A. What's your ________?
B. ....
A. Did you say ....?
B. Yes. That's right.

A. What's your last name?
B. ....
A. How do you spell that?
B. ....

Tell about yourself:
My name is ....
My address is ....
My telephone number is ....
Now interview a friend.

FAMILY MEMBERS I
가족구성원 I

A. Who is she?
B. She's my **wife**.
A. What's her name?
B. Her name is *Betty*.

A. Who is he?
B. He's my **husband**.
A. What's his name?
B. His name is *Fred*.

아내	**1.**	wife
남편	**2.**	husband
부모		**parents**
어머니	**3.**	mother
아버지	**4.**	father
자녀		**children**
딸	**5.**	daughter
아들	**6.**	son
누나 / 언니 / 여동생	**7.**	sister
형 / 오빠 / 남동생	**8.**	brother
아기	**9.**	baby
조부모		**grandparents**
할머니	**10.**	grandmother
할아버지	**11.**	grandfather
손주		**grandchildren**
손녀	**12.**	granddaughter
손자	**13.**	grandson

A. I'd like to introduce my _______.
B. Nice to meet you.
C. Nice to meet you, too.

A. What's your _______'s name?
B. His/Her name is ....

Tell about your family.
Talk about photos of family members.

FAMILY MEMBERS II

가족구성원 II

A. Who is she?
B. She's my **aunt**.
A. What's her name?
B. Her name is *Linda*.

A. Who is he?
B. He's my **uncle**.
A. What's his name?
B. His name is *Jack*.

고모 / 이모 / 백모 / 숙모 **1.** aunt
삼촌 / 백부 / 숙부 / 고모부 / 이모부 **2.** uncle
조카딸 **3.** niece
조카 **4.** nephew
사촌 **5.** cousin

장모 / 시어머니 **6.** mother-in-law
장인 / 시아버지 **7.** father-in-law
사위 **8.** son-in-law
며느리 **9.** daughter-in-law
매부 / 매형 / 처남 / 아주버니 / 시동생 **10.** brother-in-law
형수 / 처형 / 처제 / 동서 / 시누이 / 올케 **11.** sister-in-law

A. Is he/she your ________?
B. No. He's/She's my ________.
A. Oh. What's his/her name?
B. …………

A. Let me introduce my ________.
B. I'm glad to meet you.
C. Nice meeting you, too.

Tell about your relatives:
What are their names?
Where do they live?
Draw your family tree and talk about it.

북미

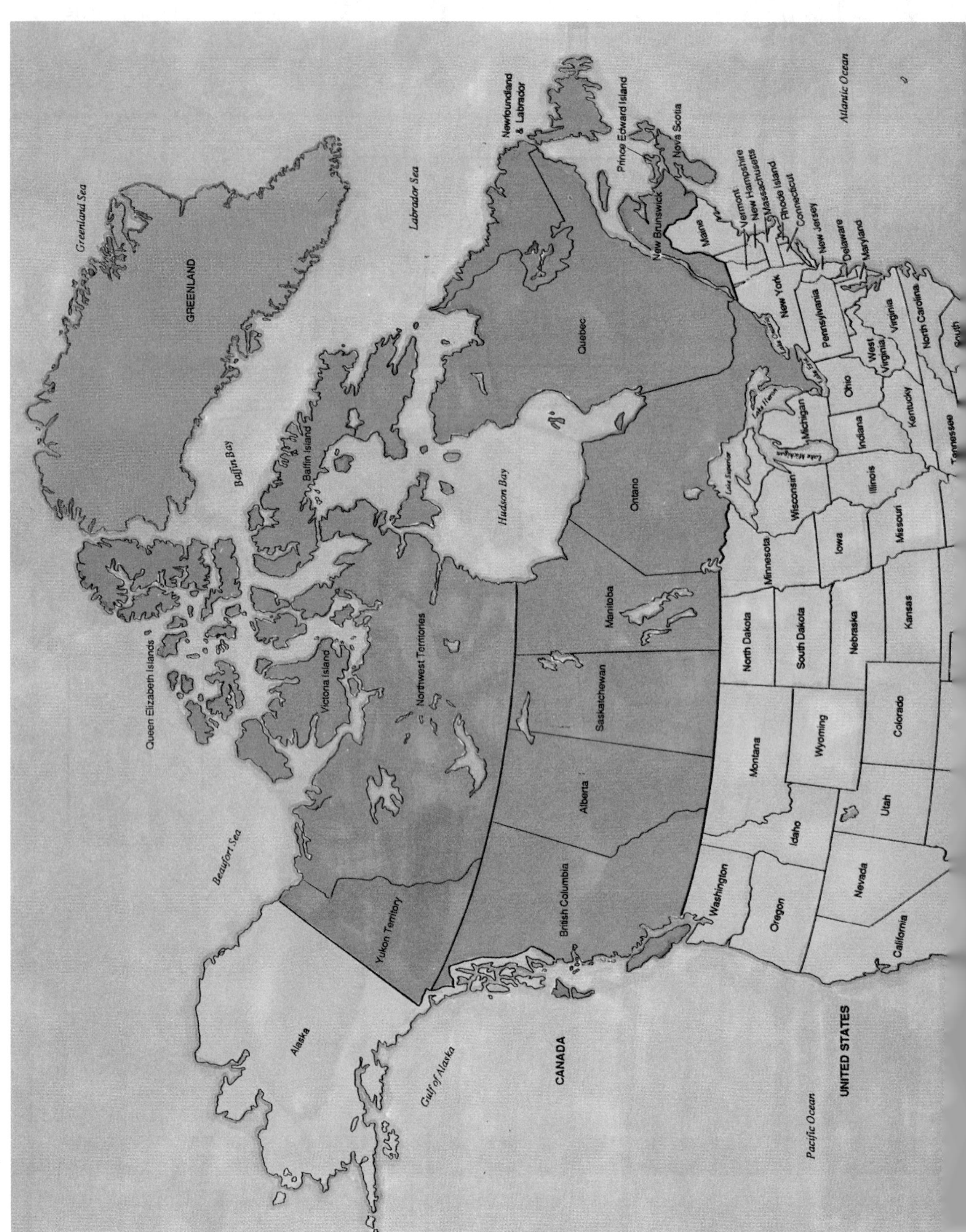
GREENLAND
Greenland Sea
Labrador Sea
Baffin Bay
Baffin Island
Hudson Bay
Queen Elizabeth Islands
Victoria Island
Northwest Territories
Beaufort Sea
Yukon Territory
Alaska
Gulf of Alaska
CANADA
British Columbia
Alberta
Saskatchewan
Manitoba
Ontario
Quebec
Newfoundland & Labrador
Prince Edward Island
Nova Scotia
New Brunswick
Maine
Vermont
New Hampshire
Massachusetts
Rhode Island
Connecticut
New Jersey
Delaware
Maryland
New York
Pennsylvania
Virginia
West Virginia
North Carolina
Ohio
Michigan
Indiana
Kentucky
Tennessee
Illinois
Wisconsin
Lake Superior
Lake Michigan
Lake Huron
Lake Ontario
Lake Erie
Minnesota
Iowa
Missouri
North Dakota
South Dakota
Nebraska
Kansas
Montana
Wyoming
Colorado
Idaho
Utah
Washington
Oregon
Nevada
California
UNITED STATES
Pacific Ocean
Atlantic Ocean

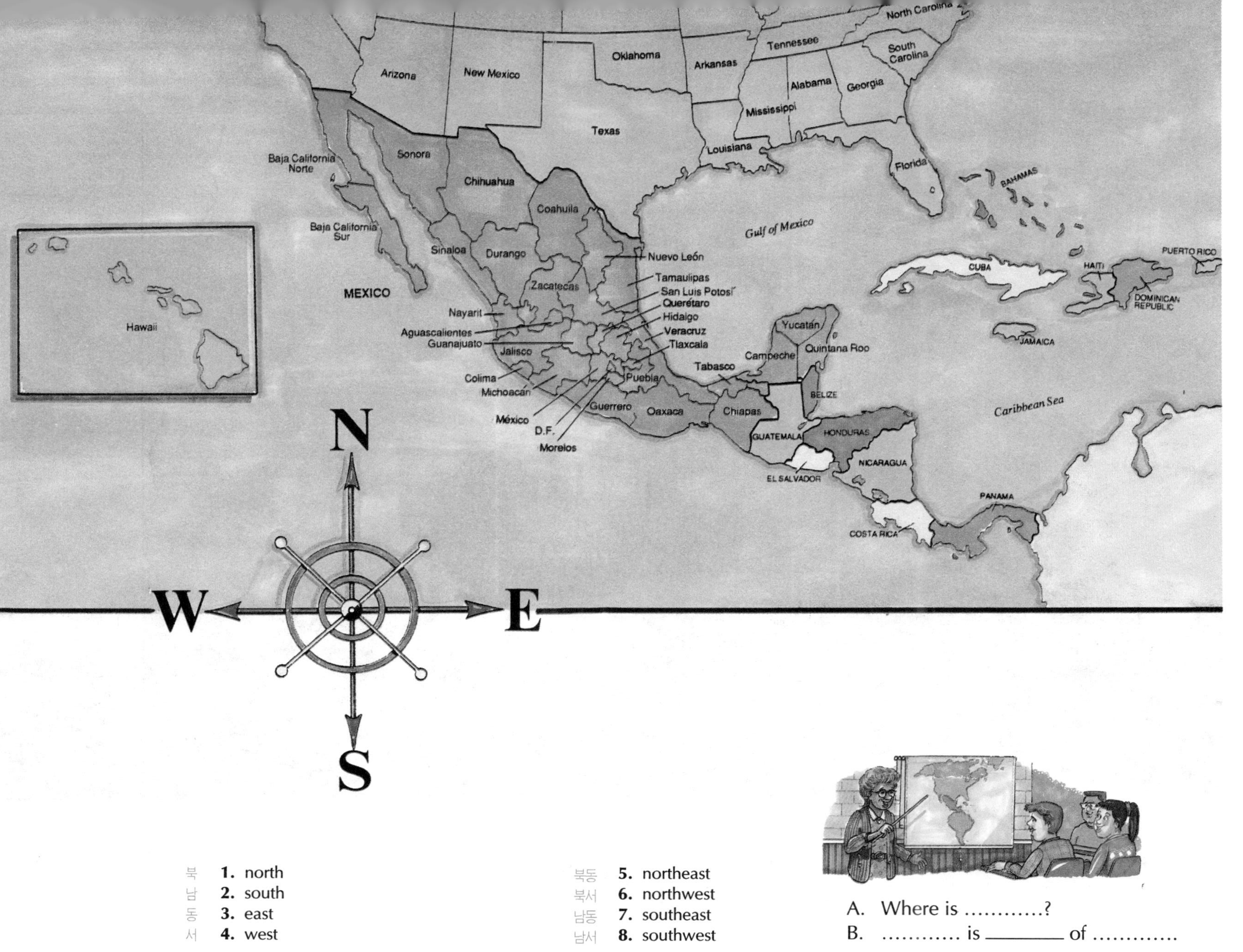

북 **1.** north
남 **2.** south
동 **3.** east
서 **4.** west

북동 **5.** northeast
북서 **6.** northwest
남동 **7.** southeast
남서 **8.** southwest

A. Where is ....?
B. .... is ________ of ....

세계

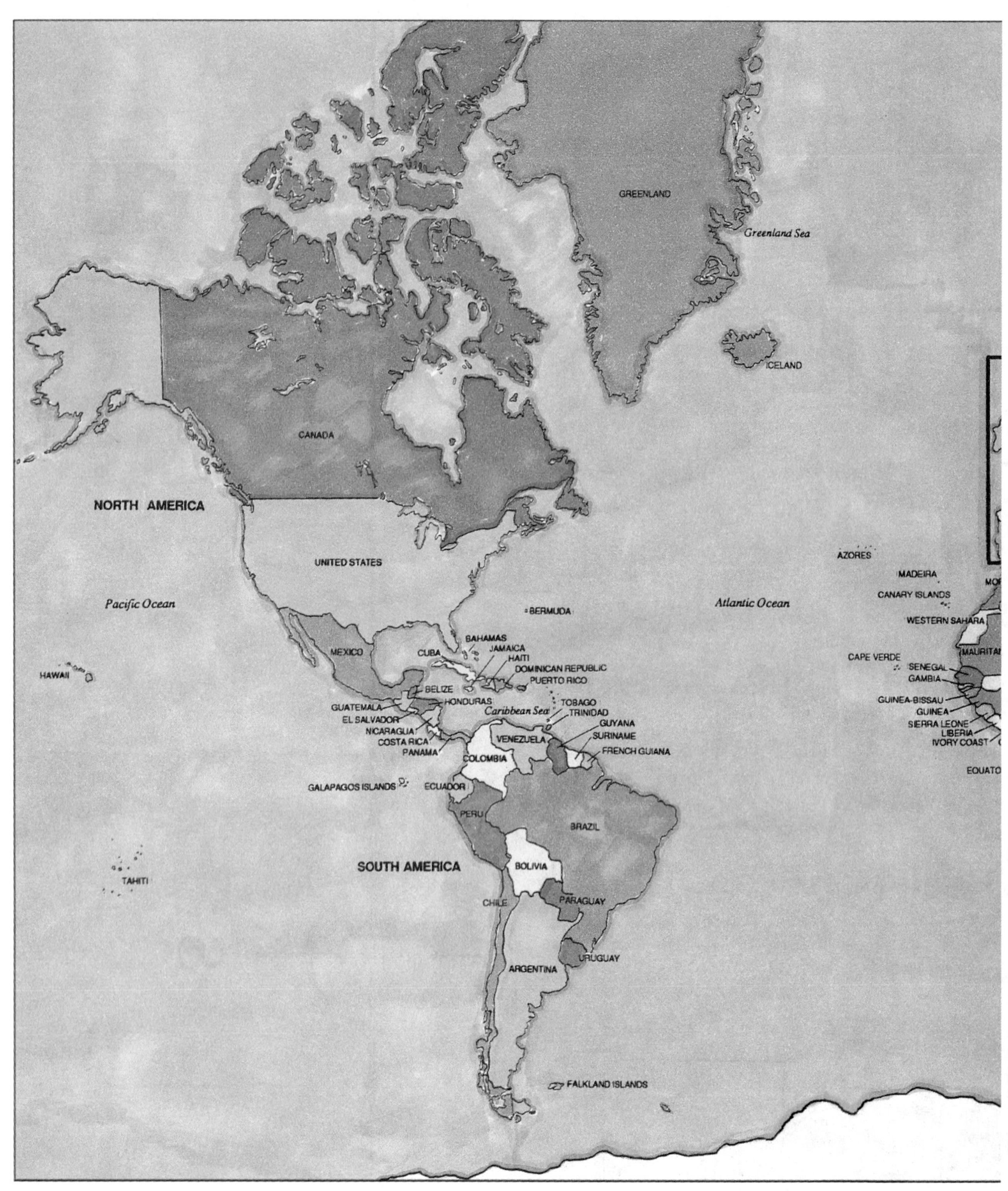

북미	**1.** North America	중동	**5.** The Middle East
남미	**2.** South America	아시아	**6.** Asia
유럽	**3.** Europe	오스트레일리아	**7.** Australia
아프리카	**4.** Africa	남극대륙	**8.** Antarctica

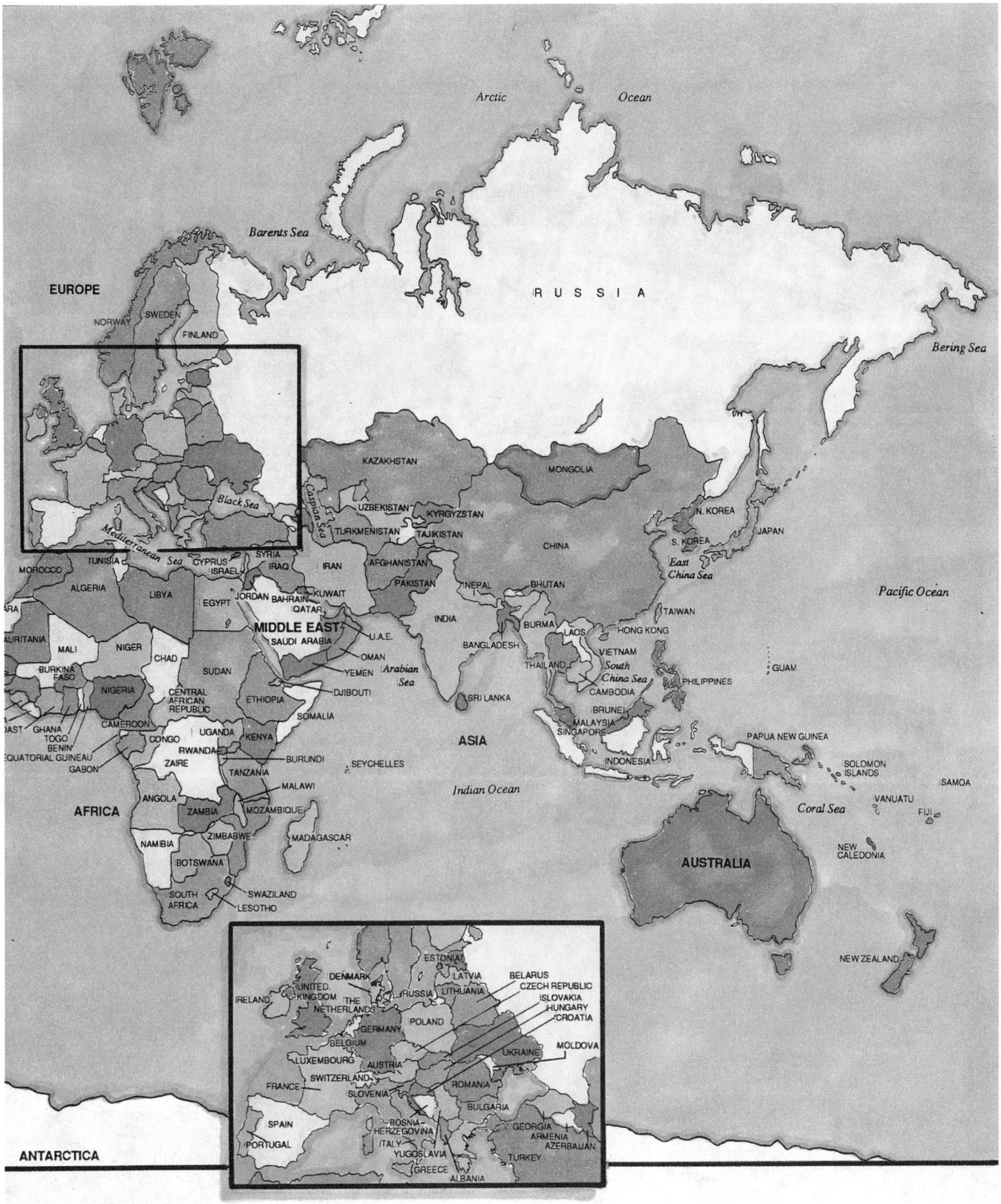

Arctic Ocean

Barents Sea

EUROPE

NORWAY SWEDEN FINLAND

RUSSIA

Bering Sea

Black Sea

Caspian Sea

Mediterranean Sea

KAZAKHSTAN MONGOLIA UZBEKISTAN KYRGYZSTAN TURKMENISTAN TAJIKISTAN N. KOREA JAPAN S. KOREA CHINA

East China Sea

Pacific Ocean

MOROCCO TUNISIA CYPRUS SYRIA IRAQ IRAN AFGHANISTAN PAKISTAN NEPAL BHUTAN ISRAEL ALGERIA LIBYA EGYPT JORDAN BAHRAIN KUWAIT QATAR TAIWAN INDIA

MIDDLE EAST

SAUDI ARABIA U.A.E. OMAN YEMEN BANGLADESH BURMA LAOS HONG KONG VIETNAM THAILAND

MALI NIGER CHAD SUDAN BURKINA FASO NIGERIA CENTRAL AFRICAN REPUBLIC ETHIOPIA DJIBOUTI SOMALIA GHANA TOGO BENIN CAMEROON EQUATORIAL GUINEAU GABON CONGO UGANDA KENYA RWANDA BURUNDI ZAIRE TANZANIA SEYCHELLES

Arabian Sea

South China Sea

CAMBODIA PHILIPPINES GUAM SRI LANKA BRUNEI MALAYSIA SINGAPORE

ASIA

PAPUA NEW GUINEA INDONESIA SOLOMON ISLANDS SAMOA

Indian Ocean

AFRICA

ANGOLA MALAWI ZAMBIA MOZAMBIQUE MADAGASCAR ZIMBABWE NAMIBIA BOTSWANA SOUTH AFRICA SWAZILAND LESOTHO

Coral Sea

VANUATU FIJI NEW CALEDONIA

AUSTRALIA

NEW ZEALAND

ESTONIA LATVIA BELARUS DENMARK UNITED KINGDOM IRELAND RUSSIA LITHUANIA CZECH REPUBLIC SLOVAKIA HUNGARY CROATIA THE NETHERLANDS POLAND GERMANY BELGIUM LUXEMBOURG AUSTRIA UKRAINE MOLDOVA SWITZERLAND FRANCE SLOVENIA ROMANIA BULGARIA SPAIN PORTUGAL BOSNIA-HERZEGOVINA ITALY YUGOSLAVIA GEORGIA ARMENIA AZERBAIJAN TURKEY GREECE ALBANIA

ANTARCTICA

A. Where's ....?
B. It's in ________.

A. What ocean/sea is near ....?

EVERYDAY ACTIVITIES I
일상활동 I

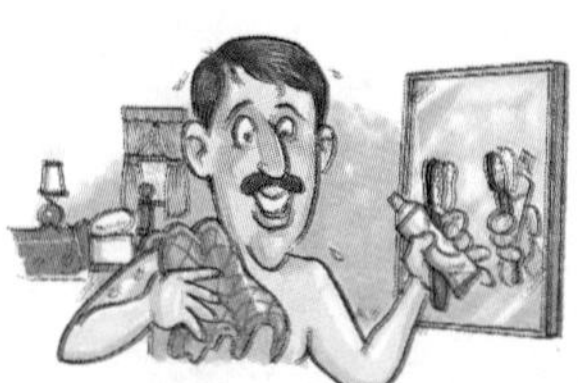

A. What do you do every day?
B. I **get up**, I **take a shower**, and I **brush my teeth**.

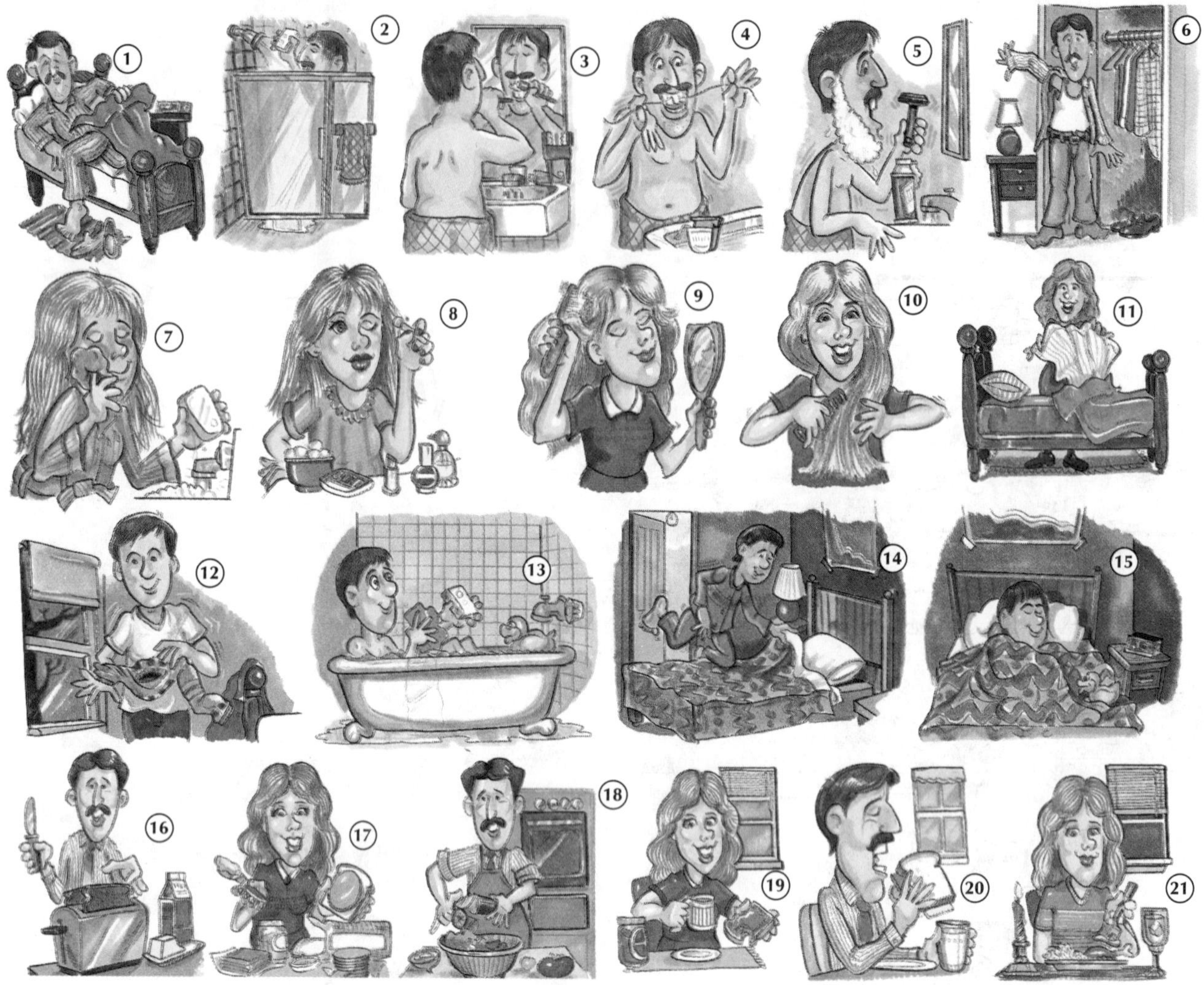

(잠에서) 일어나다 **1.** get up
샤워하다 **2.** take a shower
이를 닦다 **3.** brush my teeth
치실질하다 **4.** floss my teeth
면도하다 **5.** shave
옷을 입다 **6.** get dressed
세수하다 **7.** wash *my** face
화장하다 **8.** put on makeup
브러쉬로 머리를 빗다 **9.** brush *my** hair
빗으로 머리를 빗다 **10.** comb *my** hair
잠자리를 정돈하다 **11.** make the bed

*my, his, her, our, your, their

옷을 벗다 **12.** get undressed
목욕하다 **13.** take a bath
잠자리에 들다 **14.** go to bed
잠자다 **15.** sleep
아침식사를 준비하다 **16.** make breakfast
점심식사를 준비하다 **17.** make lunch
저녁식사를 요리하다 **18.** cook/make dinner
아침을 먹다 **19.** eat/have breakfast
점심을 먹다 **20.** eat/have lunch
저녁을 먹다 **21.** eat/have dinner

A. What does he do every day?
B. He ________s, he ________s, and he ________s.

A. What does she do every day?
B. She ________s, she ________s, and she ________s.

What do you do every day? Make a list.
Interview some friends and tell about their everyday activities.

일상활동 II

A. Hi! What are you doing?
B. I'm **clean**ing **the apartment**.

아파트를(집을) 청소하다	**1.** clean the apartment/ clean the house	텔레비전을 보다	**11.** watch TV
바닥을 쓸다	**2.** sweep the floor	라디오를 듣다	**12.** listen to the radio
먼지를 털다	**3.** dust	음악을 듣다	**13.** listen to music
진공 청소기로 청소하다	**4.** vacuum	읽다	**14.** read
설겆이하다	**5.** wash the dishes	놀다	**15.** play
빨래하다 / 세탁하다	**6.** do the laundry	농구하다	**16.** play basketball
다림질하다	**7.** iron	기타를 치다	**17.** play the guitar
아기에게 음식을 먹이다	**8.** feed the baby	피아노 연습을 하다	**18.** practice the piano
고양이에게 먹이를 주다	**9.** feed the cat	공부하다	**19.** study
개를 산책시키다	**10.** walk the dog	운동하다	**20.** exercise

A. Hi, ...! This is ....
What are you doing?
B. I'm ________ing. How about you?
A. I'm ________ing.

A. Are you going to ________ today?
B. Yes. I'm going to ________ in a little while.

What are you going to do tomorrow? Make a list of *everything* you are going to do.

THE CLASSROOM
교실

A. Where's the **teacher**?
B. The **teacher** is *next to* the **board**.

A. Where's the **pen**?
B. The **pen** is *on* the **desk**.

선생님 / 교사	**1.** teacher	칠판	**18.** board
보조교사	**2.** teacher's aide	분필 / 백묵	**19.** chalk
학생	**3.** student	칠판 턱	**20.** chalk tray
의자 / 걸상	**4.** seat/chair	칠판지우개	**21.** eraser
펜	**5.** pen	확성기 / 스피커	**22.** P.A. system/loudspeaker
연필	**6.** pencil	게시판	**23.** bulletin board
지우개	**7.** eraser	압정	**24.** thumbtack
책상	**8.** desk	지도	**25.** map
교사용 책상	**9.** teacher's desk	연필깎는 기계	**26.** pencil sharpener
책 / 교과서	**10.** book/textbook	지구본	**27.** globe
공책 / 연습장	**11.** notebook	책장	**28.** bookshelf
화일내지 / 공책지	**12.** notebook paper	오버헤드 프로젝터	**29.** overhead projector
그래프용지	**13.** graph paper	텔레비전	**30.** TV
자	**14.** ruler	(영사기용) 화면 / 스크린	**31.** (movie) screen
(전자)계산기	**15.** calculator	환등기	**32.** slide projector
시계	**16.** clock	컴퓨터	**33.** computer
국기 / 깃발	**17.** flag	영사기	**34.** (movie) projector

A. Is there a/an ________ in your classroom?*
B. Yes. There's a/an ________ next to/on the ________.

A. Is there a/an ________ in your classroom?*
B. No, there isn't.

**With 12, 13, 19 use:* Is there ________ in your classroom?

Describe your classroom.
(There's a/an ....)

수업활동

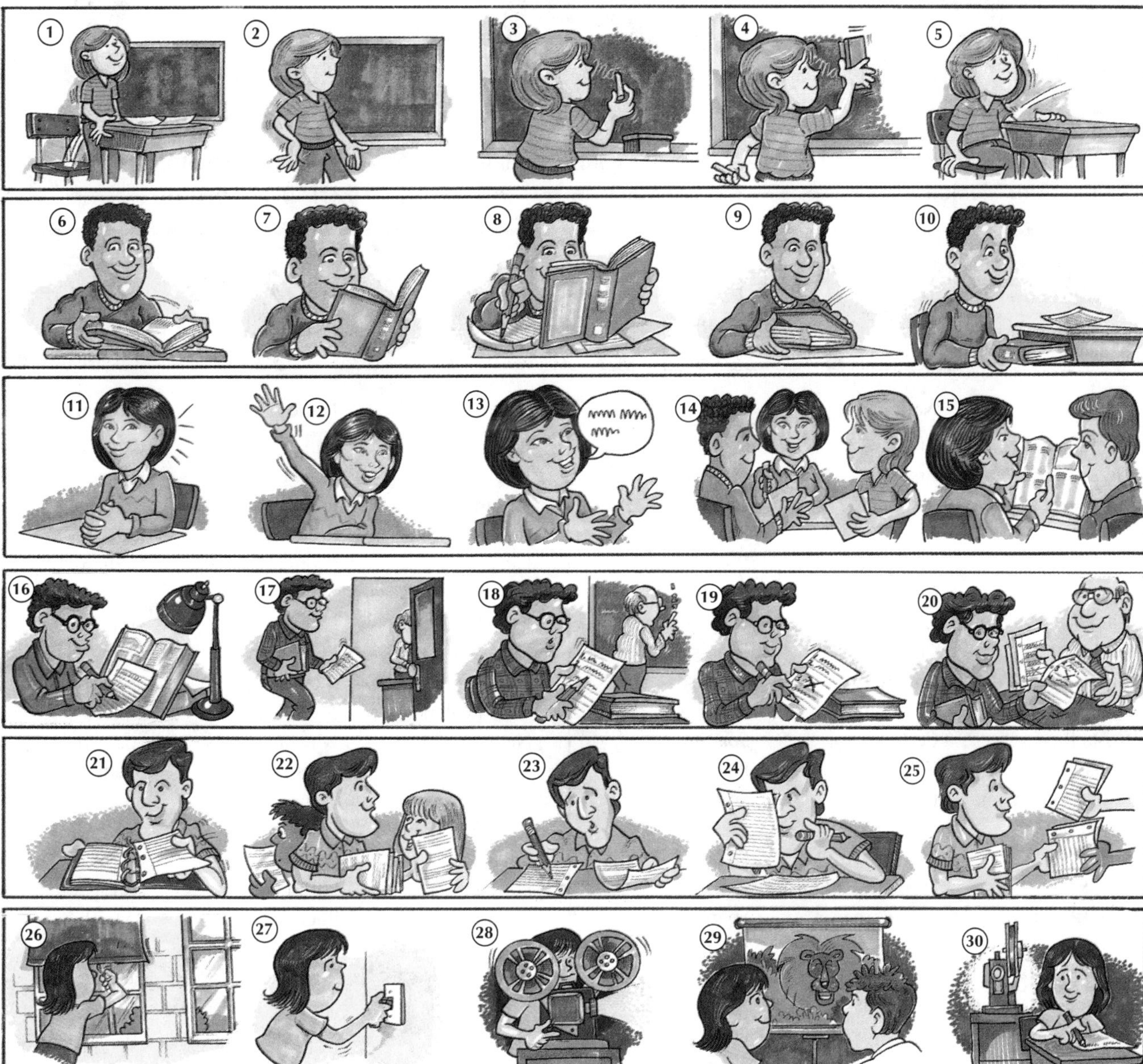

일어나세요. **1.** Stand up.
칠판으로 가세요. **2.** Go to the *board.*
자신의 이름을 쓰세요. **3.** Write *your name.*
이름을 지우세요. **4.** Erase *your name.*
앉으세요 / 자리에 앉으세요. **5.** Sit down./Take your seat.

책을 펴세요. **6.** Open *your book.*
8페이지를 읽으세요. **7.** Read *page eight.*
8페이지를 공부하세요 **8.** Study *page eight.*
책을 덮으세요. **9.** Close *your book.*
책을 치우세요. **10.** Put away *your book.*

질문을 들어보세요 **11.** Listen to *the question.*
손을 드세요. **12.** Raise *your hand.*
대답을 하세요. **13.** Give *the answer.*
그룹별로 논의하세요 **14.** Work *in groups.*
서로 도와 주세요. **15.** Help *each other.*

숙제를 하세요 **16.** Do *your homework.*
숙제를 가져 오세요 **17.** Bring in *your homework.*
답안을 검토하세요 **18.** Go over *the answers.*
틀린 답을 정정하세요 **19.** Correct *your mistakes.*
숙제를 제출하세요 **20.** Hand in *your homework.*

종이를 한 장 꺼내세요. **21.** Take out *a piece of paper.*
문제지를 돌리세요. **22.** Pass out *the tests.*
문제를 푸세요. **23.** Answer *the questions.*
답안을 확인하세요. **24.** Check *your answers.*
문제지를 거두세요. **25.** Collect *the tests.*

커튼을 내리세요 **26.** Lower *the shades.*
불을 끄세요 **27.** Turn off *the lights.*
영사기를 켜세요 **28.** Turn on *the projector.*
영화를 보세요 **29.** Watch *the movie.*
메모를 하세요 **30.** Take notes.

You're the teacher! Give instructions to your students.

국가, 국적과 언어

A. Where are you from?
B. I'm from **Mexico**.

A. What's your nationality?
B. I'm **Mexican**.

A. What language do you speak?
B. I speak **Spanish**.

      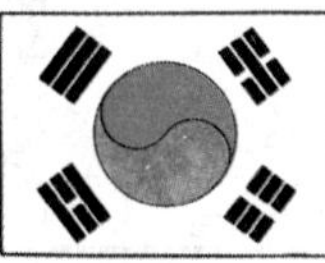 

Country	Nationality	Language
Afghanistan	Afghan	Afghan
Argentina	Argentine	Spanish
Australia	Australian	English
Bolivia	Bolivian	Spanish
Brazil	Brazilian	Portuguese
Cambodia	Cambodian	Cambodian
Canada	Canadian	English/French
Chile	Chilean	Spanish
China	Chinese	Chinese
Colombia	Colombian	Spanish
Costa Rica	Costa Rican	Spanish
Cuba	Cuban	Spanish
(The) Dominican Republic	Dominican	Spanish
Ecuador	Ecuadorian	Spanish
Egypt	Egyptian	Arabic
El Salvador	Salvadorean	Spanish
England	English	English
Estonia	Estonian	Estonian
Ethiopia	Ethiopian	Amharic
France	French	French
Germany	German	German
Greece	Greek	Greek
Guatemala	Guatemalan	Spanish
Haiti	Haitian	Haitian Kreyol
Honduras	Honduran	Spanish
Indonesia	Indonesian	Indonesian
Israel	Israeli	Hebrew
Italy	Italian	Italian
Japan	Japanese	Japanese
Jordan	Jordanian	Arabic
Korea	Korean	Korean
Laos	Laotian	Laotian
Latvia	Latvian	Latvian
Lithuania	Lithuanian	Lithuanian
Malaysia	Malaysian	Malay
Mexico	Mexican	Spanish
New Zealand	New Zealander	English
Nicaragua	Nicaraguan	Spanish
Panama	Panamanian	Spanish
Peru	Peruvian	Spanish
(The) Philippines	Filipino	Tagalog
Poland	Polish	Polish
Portugal	Portuguese	Portuguese
Puerto Rico	Puerto Rican	Spanish
Romania	Romanian	Romanian
Russia	Russian	Russian
Saudi Arabia	Saudi	Arabic
Spain	Spanish	Spanish
Taiwan	Taiwanese	Chinese
Thailand	Thai	Thai
Turkey	Turkish	Turkish
Ukraine	Ukrainian	Ukrainian
(The) United States	American	English
Venezuela	Venezuelan	Spanish
Vietnam	Vietnamese	Vietnamese

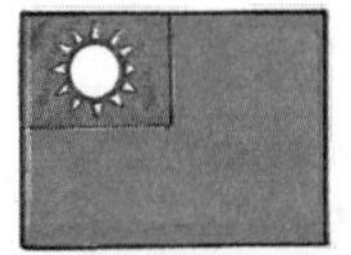 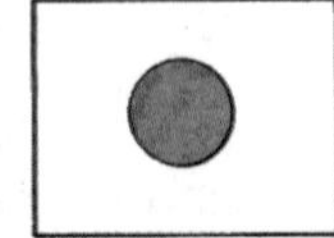     

A. What's your native language?
B. _______.
A. Oh. What country are you from?
B. _______.

A. Where are you and your husband/wife going on your vacation?
B. We're going to _______.
A. That's nice. Tell me, do you speak _______?
B. No, but my husband/wife does. He's/She's _______.

Tell about yourself:
Where are you from?
What's your nationality?
What languages do you speak?
Now interview and tell about a friend.

TYPES OF HOUSING
주거형태

A. Where do you live?
B. I live in an **apartment building**.

아파트	**1.** apartment (building)
단독주택	**2.** (single-family) house
2세대용 주택	**3.** duplex/two-family house
연립주택	**4.** townhouse/townhome
콘도미니엄 / 콘도	**5.** condominimum/condo
기숙사	**6.** dormitory/dorm
이동주택 / 트레일러	**7.** mobile home/trailer
농가	**8.** farmhouse
통나무집	**9.** cabin
양로원	**10.** nursing home
보호시설	**11.** shelter
선상주택	**12.** houseboat

A. Town Taxi Company.
B. Hello. Please send a taxi to *(address)*.
A. Is that a house or an apartment?
B. It's a/an ______.
A. All right. We'll be there right away.

A. This is the Emergency Operator.
B. Please send an ambulance to *(address)*.
A. Is that a private home?
B. It's a/an ______.
A. What's your name?
B. ....
A. And your telephone number?
B. ....

Tell about people you know and the types of housing they live in.
Discuss:
Who lives in dormitories?
Who lives in nursing homes?
Who lives in shelters?
Why?

THE LIVING ROOM
거실

A. Where are you?
B. I'm in the living room.
A. What are you doing?
B. I'm *dusting** the **coffee table**.

*dusting/cleaning

- 응접실용 탁자 **1.** coffee table
- 양탄자 / 깔개 **2.** rug
- 마루 / 바닥 **3.** floor
- 안락의자 **4.** armchair
- 소파 옆에 놓는 소형테이블 **5.** end table
- 램프 **6.** lamp
- 램프 갓 **7.** lampshade
- 창(문) **8.** window
- 커튼 **9.** drapes/curtains
- 소파 **10.** sofa/couch
- 쿠션 **11.** (throw) pillow
- 천장 **12.** ceiling
- 벽 **13.** wall
- 텔레비전 오디오 장식장 **14.** wall unit/entertainment unit
- 텔레비전 **15.** television
- 비디오 **16.** video cassette recorder/VCR
- 스테레오 전축 **17.** stereo system
- 스피커 **18.** speaker
- 2인용 소파 **19.** loveseat
- 화초 **20.** plant
- 그림 **21.** painting
- 액자 **22.** frame
- 벽난로 선반 **23.** mantel
- 벽난로 **24.** fireplace
- 벽난로 가리개 **25.** fireplace screen
- 사진 **26.** picture/photograph
- 책장 / 책꽂이 **27.** bookcase

A. You have a lovely living room!
B. Oh, thank you.
A. Your _______ is/are beautiful!
B. Thank you for saying so.

A. Uh-oh! I just spilled coffee on your _______!
B. That's okay. Don't worry about it.

Tell about your living room.
(In my living room there's ....)

THE DINING ROOM
식당

A. This **dining room table** is very nice.
B. Thank you. It was a gift from my *grandmother.**

*grandmother/grandfather/aunt/uncle/...

식탁	**1.** (dining room) table	촛대	**12.** candlestick
의자	**2.** (dining room) chair	양초	**13.** candle
장식용 찬장	**3.** china cabinet	(식탁 가운데 놓는)꽃장식	**14.** centerpiece
자기(그릇)	**4.** china	소금통	**15.** salt shaker
샹들리에	**5.** chandelier	후추통	**16.** pepper shaker
식기장	**6.** buffet	버터접시	**17.** butter dish
샐러드 용기	**7.** salad bowl	서빙카트	**18.** serving cart
주전자	**8.** pitcher	차 주전자	**19.** teapot
서빙용 용기	**9.** serving bowl	커피 주전자	**20.** coffee pot
서빙용 쟁반	**10.** serving platter	프림용기	**21.** creamer
식탁보	**11.** tablecloth	설탕용기	**22.** sugar bowl

[In a store]

A. May I help you?
B. Yes, please. Do you have ________s?*
A. Yes. ________s* are right over there.
B. Thank you.

**With 4, use the singular.*

[At home]

A. Look at this old ________ I just bought!
B. Where did you buy it?
A. At a yard sale. How do you like it?
B. It's VERY unusual!

Tell about your dining room.
(In my dining room there's ....)

THE DINING ROOM: A PLACE SETTING

식당 : 식탁 차리기

A. Excuse me. Where does the **salad plate** go?
B. It goes *to the left of* the **dinner plate**.

A. Excuse me. Where does the **soup spoon** go?
B. It goes *to the right of* the **teaspoon**.

A. Excuse me. Where does the **wine glass** go?
B. It goes *between* the **water glass** and the **cup and saucer**.

A. Excuse me. Where does the **cup** go?
B. It goes *on* the **saucer**.

샐러드용 접시	**1.** salad plate
빵접시	**2.** bread-and-butter plate
디너접시	**3.** dinner plate
수프접시	**4.** soup bowl
물잔	**5.** water glass
포도주잔	**6.** wine glass
컵 / 잔	**7.** cup
(컵)잔 받침	**8.** saucer
냅킨	**9.** napkin

식기류	**silverware**
샐러드용 포크	**10.** salad fork
식사용 포크	**11.** dinner fork
나이프	**12.** knife
티 스푼	**13.** teaspoon
수프용 스푼	**14.** soup spoon
버터 나이프	**15.** butter knife

A. Waiter? Excuse me. This _______ is dirty.
B. I'm terribly sorry. I'll get you another _______ right away.

A. Oops! I dropped my _______!
B. That's okay! I'll get you another _______ from the kitchen.

Practice giving directions. Tell someone how to set a table. (Put the ....)

THE BEDROOM

침실

A. Ooh! Look at that big bug!!
B. Where?
A. It's on the **bed**!
B. I'LL get it.

침대	**1.**	bed	거울	**18.**	mirror
침대 머리판	**2.**	headboard	보석함	**19.**	jewelry box
베개	**3.**	pillow	화장대 / 경대	**20.**	dresser/bureau
베갯잇	**4.**	pillowcase	트윈 베드	**21.**	twin bed
매트 커버	**5.**	fitted sheet	매트리스	**22.**	mattress
홑 이불	**6.**	(flat) sheet	스프링	**23.**	box spring
담요	**7.**	blanket	더블 베드	**24.**	double bed
전기 담요	**8.**	electric blanket	퀸 사이즈 베드	**25.**	queen-size bed
장식용 러플	**9.**	dust ruffle	킹 사이즈 베드	**26.**	king-size bed
침대커버	**10.**	bedspread	이층 침대	**27.**	bunk bed
이불	**11.**	comforter/quilt	트런들 베드	**28.**	trundle bed
발판	**12.**	footboard	소파 침대	**29.**	sofa bed/convertible sofa
블라인드 / 햇볕 가리개	**13.**	blinds	소파겸용 침대	**30.**	day bed
침대옆의 탁자	**14.**	night table/nightstand	간이 침대	**31.**	cot
자명종	**15.**	alarm clock	물침대	**32.**	water bed
시계 라디오	**16.**	clock radio	천장 달린 침대	**33.**	canopy bed
서랍장	**17.**	chest (of drawers)	병원 침대	**34.**	hospital bed

[In a store]

A. Excuse me. I'm looking for a/an _______.*
B. We have some very nice _______s. And they're all on sale this week.
A. Oh, good!

With 13, use: Excuse me. I'm looking for _______.

[In a bedroom]

A. Oh, no! I just lost my contact lens!
B. Where?
A. I think it's on the _______.
B. I'll help you look.

Tell about your bedroom.
(In my bedroom there's ....)

THE KITCHEN
부엌

A. I think we need a new **dishwasher**.
B. I think you're right.

식기 세척기	**1.** dishwasher
식기 세척기용 세제	**2.** dishwasher detergent
주방용 세제	**3.** dishwashing liquid
수도꼭지	**4.** faucet
개수대	**5.** (kitchen) sink
오물 분쇄기	**6.** (garbage) disposal
스폰지	**7.** sponge
수세미	**8.** scouring pad
남비 닦는 기구	**9.** pot scrubber
식기 건조대	**10.** dish rack
종이 타올걸이	**11.** paper towel holder
행주	**12.** dish towel
쓰레기 압축기	**13.** trash compactor
찬장	**14.** cabinet
전자레인지	**15.** microwave (oven)
조리대	**16.** (kitchen) counter
도마	**17.** cutting board
설탕, 커피등을 보관하는 용기	**18.** canister
가스 레인지	**19.** stove/range
버너	**20.** burner
오븐	**21.** oven
남비집게	**22.** potholder
토스터기	**23.** toaster
양념통 보관대	**24.** spice rack
깡통따개	**25.** (electric) can opener
요리책	**26.** cookbook
냉장고	**27.** refrigerator
냉동실	**28.** freezer
제빙기	**29.** ice maker
얼음그릇	**30.** ice tray
냉장고에 붙이는 장식용 자석	**31.** refrigerator magnet
(부엌내) 간이식탁	**32.** kitchen table
식탁매트	**33.** placemat
부엌용 의자	**34.** kitchen chair
쓰레기통	**35.** garbage pail

[In a store]
A. Excuse me. Are your ________s still on sale?
B. Yes, they are. They're twenty percent off.

[In a kitchen]
A. When did you get this/these new ________(s)?
B. I got it/them last week.

Tell about your kitchen.
(In my kitchen there's ....)

KITCHENWARE
주방용품

A. Could I possibly borrow your **wok**?
B. Sure. I'll get it for you right now.
A. Thanks.

중국남비	**1.**	wok
남비 / 솥	**2.**	pot
스튜용 남비	**3.**	saucepan
뚜껑	**4.**	lid/cover/top
프라이팬	**5.**	frying pan/skillet
오븐용 구이판	**6.**	roasting pan
로스터	**7.**	roaster
이중남비	**8.**	double boiler
압력솥	**9.**	pressure cooker
물 거르개	**10.**	colander
찜남비	**11.**	casserole (dish)
케익 굽는 용기	**12.**	cake pan
파이 굽는 용기	**13.**	pie plate
과자 굽는 판	**14.**	cookie sheet
믹싱 보울	**15.**	(mixing) bowl
밀대 / 밀방망이	**16.**	rolling pin
계량컵	**17.**	measuring cup
계량스푼	**18.**	measuring spoon
원두커피 끓이는 기구	**19.**	coffeemaker
원두커피 분쇄기	**20.**	coffee grinder
차 주전자	**21.**	tea kettle
토스터기	**22.**	toaster oven
(전기) 혼합기	**23.**	(electric) mixer
만능 조리기구	**24.**	food processor
전기 프라이팬	**25.**	electric frying pan
와플 굽는 기구	**26.**	waffle iron
전기 프라이팬	**27.**	(electric) griddle
팝콘 제조기	**28.**	popcorn maker
믹서기	**29.**	blender
강판	**30.**	grater
(계란) 거품기	**31.**	(egg) beater
국자	**32.**	ladle
아이스크림 떠내는 스푼	**33.**	ice cream scoop
과자 모양내는 틀	**34.**	cookie cutter
체	**35.**	strainer
마늘 찧는 기구	**36.**	garlic press
병따개	**37.**	bottle opener
깡통따개	**38.**	can opener
(계란) 거품기	**39.**	whisk
야채 껍질 깎는 기구	**40.**	(vegetable) peeler
칼	**41.**	knife
(프라이팬) 뒤집개	**42.**	spatula
과도	**43.**	paring knife

A. What are you looking for?
B. I'm looking for the ________.*
A. Did you look in the drawers/in the cabinets/next to the ________/............?
B. Yes. I looked everywhere!

*With 2, 4, 12–15, 41, use: I'm looking for a ________.

[A Commercial]

Come to *Kitchen World*! We have everything you need for your kitchen, from ________s and ________s, to ________s and ________s. Are you looking for a new ________? Is it time to throw out your old ________? Come to *Kitchen World* today! We have everything you need!

What things do you have in your kitchen?
Which things do you use very often?
Which things do you rarely use?

THE BABY'S ROOM
아가방

A. Thank you for the **teddy bear.** It's a very nice gift.
B. You're welcome. Tell me, when are you due?
A. In a few more weeks.

곰인형	**1.**	teddy bear
인터폰	**2.**	intercom
서랍장	**3.**	chest (of drawers)
아기침대	**4.**	crib
아기침대 난간	**5.**	crib bumper
모빌	**6.**	mobile
아기침대용 장난감	**7.**	crib toy
야간등	**8.**	night light
기저귀 테이블	**9.**	changing table/ dressing table
유아용 우주복	**10.**	stretch suit
기저귀 테이블 패드	**11.**	changing pad
기저귀 쓰레기통	**12.**	diaper pail
장난감 상자	**13.**	toy chest
인형	**14.**	doll
그네	**15.**	swing
플래이 팬 / 유아용 놀이공간	**16.**	playpen
봉제인형	**17.**	stuffed animal
딸랑이	**18.**	rattle
흔들침대	**19.**	cradle
보행기	**20.**	walker
유아용 안전의자	**21.**	car seat
간이 유모차	**22.**	stroller
유모차	**23.**	baby carriage
보온용기	**24.**	food warmer
보조의자 / 부스터 체어	**25.**	booster seat
아기의자	**26.**	baby seat
유아용 식사의자	**27.**	high chair
유아용 이동침대	**28.**	portable crib
아기 업는 띠	**29.**	baby carrier
유아용 변기	**30.**	potty

A. That's a very nice _______.
Where did you get it?
B. It was a gift from ....

A. Do you have everything you need before the baby comes?
B. Almost everything. We're still looking for a/an _______ and a/an _______.

Tell about your country:
What things do people buy for a new baby?
Does a new baby sleep in a separate room, as in the United States?

육아용품

[1–12]
A. Do we need anything from the store?
B. Yes. Could you get some more **baby powder**?
A. Sure.

[13–17]
A. Do we need anything from the store?
B. Yes. Could you get another **pacifier**?
A. Sure.

땀띠분	**1.** baby powder
유아용 로션	**2.** baby lotion
유아용 샴푸	**3.** baby shampoo
연고	**4.** ointment
분유	**5.** formula
이유식	**6.** baby food
물휴지	**7.** (baby) wipes
면봉	**8.** cotton swabs
기저귀용 옷핀	**9.** diaper pins
일회용 기저귀	**10.** disposable diapers
천 기저귀	**11.** cloth diapers
(액체) 비타민	**12.** (liquid) vitamins
노리개 젖꼭지	**13.** pacifier
젖병 / 우유병	**14.** bottle
(젖병의) 고무젖꼭지	**15.** nipple
턱받이	**16.** bib
치아발육기	**17.** teething ring

[In a store]
A. Excuse me. I can't find the ________.*
B. I'm sorry. We're out of ________.* We'll have some more tomorrow.

[At home]
A. Honey? Where did you put the ________?
B. It's/They're in/on/next to the ________.

With 13–17, use the plural.

In your opinion, which are better: cloth diapers or disposable diapers? Why?
Tell about baby products in your country.

THE BATHROOM
욕실

A. Where's the **plunger**?
B. It's *next to* the **toilet**.

A. Where's the **toothbrush**?
B. It's *in* the **toothbrush holder**.

A. Where's the **washcloth**?
B. It's *on* the **towel rack**.

A. Where's the **mirror**?
B. It's *over* the **sink**.

배수관 흡착 청소막대	**1.** plunger	선반	**15.** shelf	물비누통	**28.** soap dispenser
변기	**2.** toilet	헤어 드라이기	**16.** hair dryer	워터픽 / 치아청소기	**29.** Water Pik
변기 물탱크	**3.** toilet tank	환풍기	**17.** fan	욕실 화장대 / 수건장	**30.** vanity
변기 시트	**4.** toilet seat	거울	**18.** mirror	쓰레기통	**31.** wastebasket
방향제	**5.** air freshener	약장	**19.** medicine cabinet/ medicine chest	샤워실	**32.** shower
화장지 걸이	**6.** toilet paper holder			샤워 커튼 봉	**33.** shower curtain rod
두루마리 화장지	**7.** toilet paper	세면대	**20.** (bathroom) sink	샤워기	**34.** shower head
변기 청소용 솔	**8.** toilet brush	온수 수도꼭지	**21.** hot water faucet	커튼 고리	**35.** shower curtain rings
수건 걸이	**9.** towel rack	냉수 수도꼭지	**22.** cold water faucet	샤워 커튼	**36.** shower curtain
목욕 수건	**10.** bath towel	컵	**23.** cup	욕조	**37.** bathtub/tub
수건	**11.** hand towel	칫솔	**24.** toothbrush	배수구	**38.** drain
작은 수건	**12.** washcloth/facecloth	칫솔걸이	**25.** toothbrush holder	욕조용 고무매트	**39.** rubber mat
세탁물 광주리	**13.** hamper	비누	**26.** soap	스폰지	**40.** sponge
체중계	**14.** (bathroom) scale	비누 받침대	**27.** soap dish	욕실 매트	**41.** bath mat/bath rug

A. [Knock. Knock.] Did I leave my glasses in there?
B. Yes. They're on/in/next to the ________.

A. *Bobby?*
B. Yes, Mom/Dad?
A. You didn't clean up the bathroom! There's toothpaste on the ________ and there's powder all over the ________!
B. Sorry, Mom/Dad. I'll clean it up right away.

Tell about your bathroom.
(In my bathroom there's ....)

PERSONAL CARE PRODUCTS
개인 위생용품

[1–17]
A. Excuse me. Where can I find **toothbrush**es?
B. They're in the next aisle.
A. Thank you.

[18–38]
A. Excuse me. Where can I find **shampoo**?
B. It's in the next aisle.
A. Thank you.

칫솔 **1.** toothbrush
빗 **2.** comb
브러쉬 **3.** (hair) brush
면도기 **4.** razor
면도날 **5.** razor blades
전기 면도기 **6.** electric razor/ electric shaver
지혈봉 **7.** styptic pencil
샤워 캡 **8.** shower cap
줄칼 **9.** nail file
줄칼 **10.** emery board
손톱깎이 **11.** nail clipper
손톱솔 **12.** nail brush
가위 **13.** scissors
쪽집게 **14.** tweezers

실핀 **15.** bobby pins
머리집게 **16.** hair clips
머리핀 **17.** barrettes
샴푸 **18.** shampoo
린스 **19.** conditioner/rinse
헤어스프레이 **20.** hairspray
치약 **21.** toothpaste
구강청정액 / 구강청결제 **22.** mouthwash
플로스 / 치실 **23.** dental floss
쉐이브 크림 **24.** shaving creme
쉐이브 로션 **25.** after shave lotion
디오도런트 / 방취제 **26.** deodorant
땀띠분 **27.** powder
핸드 로션 **28.** hand lotion
향수 **29.** perfume/cologne

구두약 **30.** shoe polish
매니큐어 **31.** nail polish
매니큐어 제거제 **32.** nail polish remover

화장용품 makeup
파운데이션 **33.** base/foundation
볼연지 **34.** blush/rouge
립스틱 **35.** lipstick
아이섀도우 **36.** eye shadow
아이라이너 **37.** eye liner
마스카라 **38.** mascara

A. I'm going to the drug store to get a/an ________.*
B. While you're there, could you also get a/an ________?*
A. Sure.

*With 5, 13–38, use: get ________.

A. Do you have everything for the trip?
B. I think so.
A. Did you remember to pack your ________?
B. Oops! I forgot. Thanks for reminding me.

You're going on a trip. Make a list of personal care products you need to take with you.

HOUSEHOLD CLEANING AND LAUNDRY

집안청소와 빨래

[1–17, 28–39]
A. Excuse me. Do you sell **broom**s?
B. Yes. They're at the back of the store.
A. Thanks.

[18–27]
A. Excuse me. Do you sell **laundry detergent**?
B. Yes. It's at the back of the store.
A. Thanks.

자루비	1.	broom
쓰레받기	2.	dustpan
비	3.	whisk broom
총채	4.	feather duster
걸레	5.	dust cloth
다리미	6.	iron
다림질 판	7.	ironing board
양탄자 청소기	8.	carpet sweeper
진공 청소기	9.	vacuum (cleaner)
진공 청소기 부속품	10.	vacuum cleaner attachments
먼지 주머니	11.	vacuum cleaner bag
휴대용 진공 청소기	12.	hand vacuum
자루걸레	13.	(dust) mop/ (dry) mop
스폰지 걸레	14.	(sponge) mop
젖은 걸레	15.	(wet) mop
세탁기	16.	washing machine/ washer
빨래 건조기	17.	dryer
세탁세제	18.	laundry detergent
섬유 유연제	19.	fabric softener
표백제	20.	bleach
다림풀	21.	starch
정전기 제거제	22.	static cling remover
세제	23.	cleanser
유리닦는 세제	24.	window cleaner
암모니아	25.	ammonia
가구 광택제	26.	furniture polish
마루용 왁스	27.	floor wax
종이 타올	28.	paper towels
옷걸이	29.	hanger
세탁물 광주리	30.	laundry basket
세탁물 가방	31.	laundry bag
다용도 싱크	32.	utility sink
세탁솔	33.	scrub brush
스폰지	34.	sponge
양동이	35.	bucket/pail
쓰레기통	36.	trash can/ garbage can
재활용 상자	37.	recycling bin
빨랫줄	38.	clothesline
빨래집게	39.	clothespins

A. How do you like this/these ______?
B. It's/They're great!

A. They're having a big sale at Dave's Discount Store this week.
B. Oh, really? What's on sale?
A. [18–27] and [1–17, 28–39] s.

Who does the cleaning and laundry in your home? What things does that person use?

옥외

A. When are you going to repair the **lamppost**?
B. I'm going to repair it next Saturday.

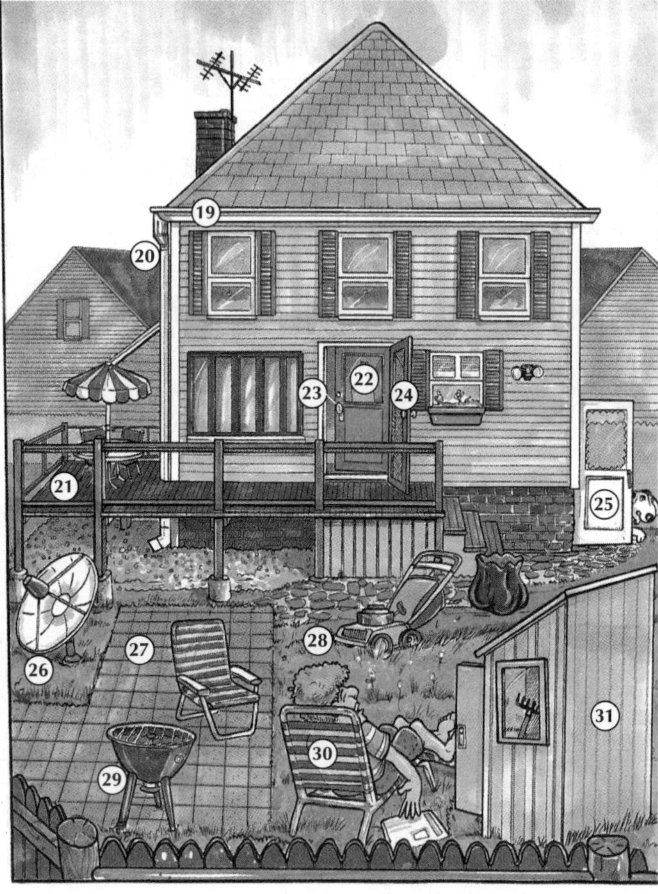

가로등기둥	**1.** lamppost		차고 문	**17.** garage door
우편함	**2.** mailbox		차도	**18.** driveway
현관 앞길	**3.** front walk		홈통 / 처마 물받이	**19.** gutter
현관 계단	**4.** front steps		배수관	**20.** drainpipe/downspout
현관	**5.** (front) porch		데크	**21.** deck
현관 덧문	**6.** storm door		뒷문	**22.** back door
현관문	**7.** front door		손잡이	**23.** doorknob
초인종	**8.** doorbell		방충문	**24.** screen door
현관등	**9.** (front) light		옆문	**25.** side door
창문	**10.** window		위성방송 수신기	**26.** satellite dish
방충망	**11.** (window) screen		안뜰	**27.** patio
덧문 / 셔터	**12.** shutter		잔디 깎는 기계	**28.** lawnmower
지붕	**13.** roof		바베큐용 석쇠	**29.** barbecue/(outdoor) grill
텔레비전 안테나	**14.** TV antenna		야외용 의자	**30.** lawn chair
굴뚝	**15.** chimney		연장(보관)창고	**31.** tool shed
차고	**16.** garage			

[On the telephone]

A. Harry's Home Repairs.
B. Hello. Do you fix ________s?
A. No, we don't.
B. Oh, okay. Thank you.

[At work on Monday morning]

A. What did you do this weekend?
B. Nothing much. I repaired my ________ and my ________.

Do you like to repair things?
What things can you repair yourself?
What things can't you repair? Who repairs them?

THE APARTMENT BUILDING

아파트

A. Is there a **lobby**?
B. Yes, there is. Do you want to see the apartment?
A. Yes, I do.

로비	**1.** lobby	화재 경보기	**12.** fire alarm
인터폰	**2.** intercom	쓰레기 투입구	**13.** garbage chute
초인종	**3.** buzzer	세탁실	**14.** laundry room
우편함	**4.** mailbox	아파트 관리인	**15.** superintendent
승강기 / 엘리베이터	**5.** elevator	창고	**16.** storage room
수위	**6.** doorman	차고 / 옥내 주차장	**17.** parking garage
연기 탐지기	**7.** smoke detector	주차장	**18.** parking lot
방문객 확인창	**8.** peephole	발코니 / 테라스	**19.** balcony/terrace
도어 체인	**9.** (door) chain	수영장	**20.** swimming pool
잠금쇠	**10.** dead-bolt lock	수압식 목욕탕	**21.** whirlpool
에어컨	**11.** air conditioner		

[Renting an apartment]
A. Let me show you around the building.*
B. Okay.
A. This is the _______ and here's the _______.
B. I see.

**With 7–11, use:*
Let me show you around the apartment.

[On the telephone]
A. Mom and Dad? I found an apartment.
B. Good. Tell us about it.
A. It has a/an _______ and a/an _______.
B. That's nice. Does it have a/an _______?
A. Yes, it does.

Tell about the differences between living in a house and in an apartment building.

HOUSING UTILITIES, SERVICES, AND REPAIRS
주거비, 주택관리 및 보수

A. Did you remember to pay the **carpenter**?
B. Yes. I wrote a check yesterday.

목수 **1.** carpenter
잡역부 **2.** handyman
페인트공 **3.** (house) painter
굴뚝 청소부 **4.** chimney sweep
가전제품 수리공 **5.** appliance repair person
텔레비전 수리공 **6.** TV repair person
자물쇠 수리공 / 열쇠 수리공 **7.** locksmith
정원사 **8.** gardener
전기 기사 **9.** electrician
배관공 **10.** plumber
방역원 **11.** exterminator

가스요금 청구서 **12.** gas bill
전기요금 청구서 **13.** electric bill
전화요금 청구서 **14.** telephone bill
수도요금 청구서 **15.** water bill
연료비 청구서 **16.** oil bill/heating bill
케이블 텔레비전 수신료 청구서 **17.** cable TV bill
방역요금 청구서 **18.** pest control bill
임대료 **19.** rent
주차료 **20.** parking fee
주택융자 상환금 **21.** mortgage payment

[1–11]
A. When is the ________ going to come?
B. This afternoon.

[12–21]
A. When is the ________ due?
B. It's due at the end of the month.

Tell about utilities, services, and repairs you pay for. How much do you pay?

TOOLS
공구

A. Could I borrow your **hammer***?
B. Sure.
A. Thanks.

**With 28–32, use:* Could I borrow some ________s?

망치 **1.** hammer
일자 드라이버 **2.** screwdriver
십자 드라이버 **3.** Phillips screwdriver
렌치 **4.** wrench
집게 **5.** pliers
활톱 / 쇠톱 **6.** hacksaw
도끼 **7.** hatchet
멍키 렌치 **8.** monkey wrench
톱 **9.** saw
드릴 **10.** hand drill
타래송곳 **11.** brace

끌 / 정 **12.** chisel
스크레이퍼 **13.** scraper
바이스 **14.** vise
전기드릴 / 천공기 **15.** electric drill
(전기 드릴용) 날 **16.** (drill) bit
전기톱 **17.** power saw
수평기 **18.** level
대패 **19.** plane
공구상자 / 연장상자 **20.** toolbox
(페인트) 팬 **21.** (paint) pan
(페인트) 롤러 **22.** (paint) roller

페인트 솔 **23.** paintbrush/brush
페인트 **24.** paint
신나 **25.** paint thinner
샌드페이퍼 / 사포 **26.** sandpaper
철사 / 전선 **27.** wire
못 **28.** nail
나사못 **29.** screw
와셔 / 또아리쇠 **30.** washer
볼트 **31.** bolt
너트 **32.** nut

[1–4, 6–27]
A. Where's the ________?
B. It's on/next to/near/over/under the ________.

[5, 28–32]
A. Where are the ________(s)?
B. They're on/next to/near/over/under the ________.

Do you like to work with tools? What tools do you have in your home?

GARDENING TOOLS AND HOME SUPPLIES

정원용구 및 가정용품

[1–16]
A. I can't find the **lawnmower**!
B. Look in the tool shed.
A. I did.
B. Oh! Wait a minute! I lent the **lawnmower** to the neighbors.

[17–32]
A. I can't find the **flashlight**!
B. Look in the utility cabinet.
A. I did.
B. Oh! Wait a minute! I lent the **flashlight** to the neighbors.

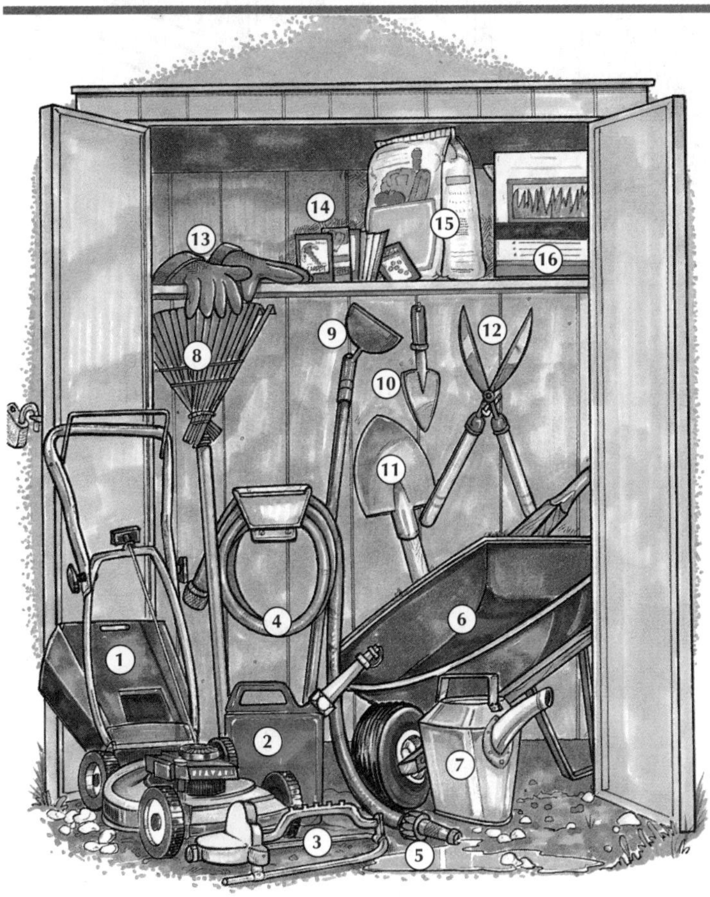

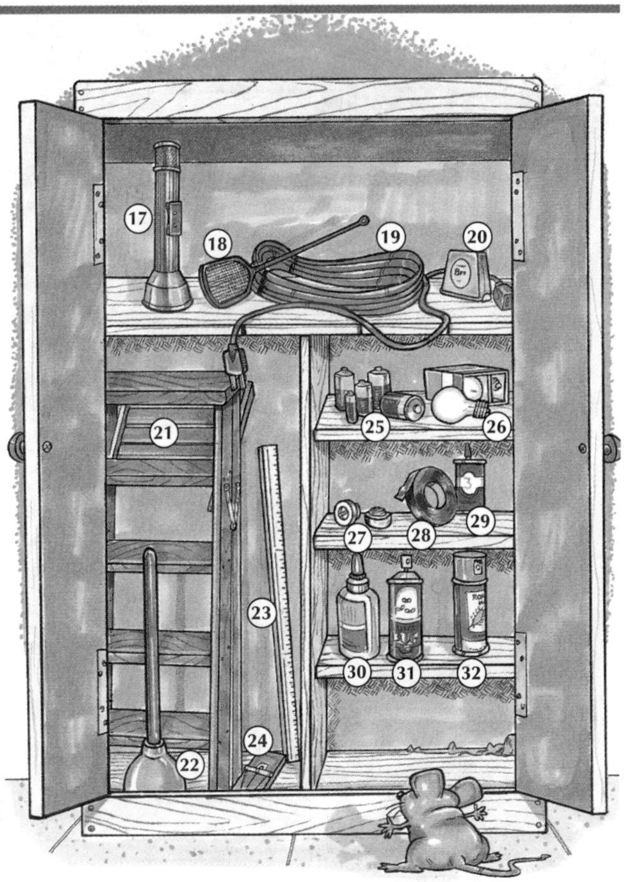

잔디 깎는 기계	**1.**	lawnmower
휘발유통	**2.**	gas can
살수기 / 스프링클러	**3.**	sprinkler
정원용 호스	**4.**	(garden) hose
노즐	**5.**	nozzle
외바퀴 손수레	**6.**	wheelbarrow
물뿌리개	**7.**	watering can
갈퀴 / 써레	**8.**	rake
괭이	**9.**	hoe
흙손	**10.**	trowel
삽	**11.**	shovel
전지가위 / 정원용 긴가위	**12.**	hedge clippers
작업용 장갑	**13.**	work gloves
야채 종자	**14.**	vegetable seeds
비료	**15.**	fertilizer
잔디 씨	**16.**	grass seed
손전등	**17.**	flashlight
파리채	**18.**	fly swatter
전기코드선 / 엑스텐션 코드	**19.**	extension cord
줄자	**20.**	tape measure
접사다리	**21.**	step ladder
배수관 흡착청소막대	**22.**	plunger
막대자	**23.**	yardstick
쥐덫	**24.**	mousetrap
건전지	**25.**	batteries
전구	**26.**	lightbulbs/bulbs
퓨즈	**27.**	fuses
전선 테이프	**28.**	electrical tape
오일	**29.**	oil
접착제 / 본드	**30.**	glue
살충제	**31.**	bug spray/ insect spray
바퀴벌레약	**32.**	roach killer

[1–11, 17–24]
A. I'm going to the hardware store. Can you think of anything we need?
B. Yes. We need a/an ________.
A. Oh, that's right.

[12–16, 25–32]
A. I'm going to the hardware store. Can you think of anything we need?
B. Yes. We need ________.
A. Oh, that's right.

What gardening tools and home supplies do you have? Tell about how and when you use each one.

NUMBERS
숫자

기수 / Cardinal Numbers

1	one	11	eleven	21	twenty-one	101	one hundred (and) one
2	two	12	twelve	22	twenty-two	102	one hundred (and) two
3	three	13	thirteen	30	thirty	1,000	one thousand
4	four	14	fourteen	40	forty	10,000	ten thousand
5	five	15	fifteen	50	fifty	100,000	one hundred thousand
6	six	16	sixteen	60	sixty	1,000,000	one million
7	seven	17	seventeen	70	seventy		
8	eight	18	eighteen	80	eighty		
9	nine	19	nineteen	90	ninety		
10	ten	20	twenty	100	one hundred		

A. How old are you?
B. I'm _______ years old.

A. How many people are there in your family?
B. _______.

서수 / Ordinal Numbers

1st	first	11th	eleventh	21st	twenty-first	101st	one hundred (and) first
2nd	second	12th	twelfth	22nd	twenty-second	102nd	one hundred (and) second
3rd	third	13th	thirteenth	30th	thirtieth	1000th	one thousandth
4th	fourth	14th	fourteenth	40th	fortieth	10,000th	ten thousandth
5th	fifth	15th	fifteenth	50th	fiftieth	100,000th	one hundred thousandth
6th	sixth	16th	sixteenth	60th	sixtieth	1,000,000th	one millionth
7th	seventh	17th	seventeenth	70th	seventieth		
8th	eighth	18th	eighteenth	80th	eightieth		
9th	ninth	19th	nineteenth	90th	ninetieth		
10th	tenth	20th	twentieth	100th	one hundredth		

A. What floor do you live on?
B. I live on the _______ floor.

A. Is this the first time you've seen this movie?
B. No. It's the _______ time.

수학

산수 / Arithmetic

더하기 addition	빼기 subtraction	곱하기 multiplication	나누기 division
2 **plus** 1 **equals*** 3.	8 **minus** 3 **equals*** 5.	4 **times** 2 **equals*** 8.	10 **divided by** 2 **equals*** 5.

You can also say:* **is

A. How much is *two plus one*?
B. *Two plus one* equals/is *three.*

Make conversations for the arithmetic problems above and others.

분수 / Fractions

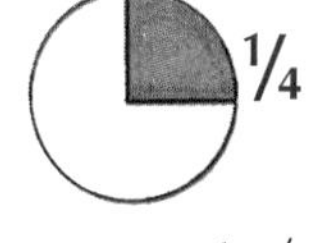

one quarter/ one fourth

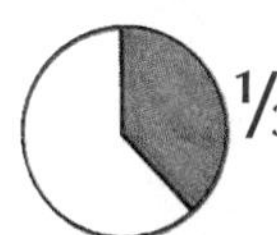

one third

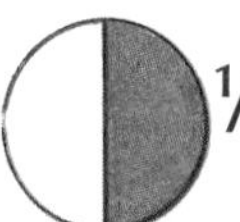

one half/ half

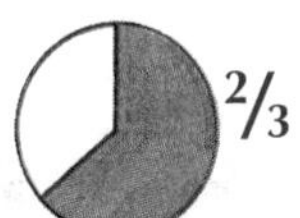

two thirds

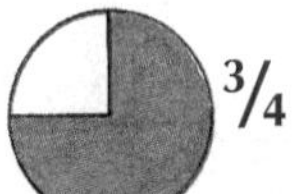

three quarters/ three fourths

A. Is this on sale?
B. Yes. It's ________ off the regular price.

A. Is the gas tank almost empty?
B. It's about ________ full.

퍼센트 / Percents

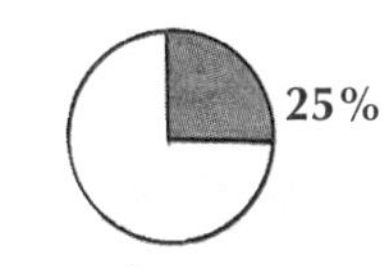

twenty-five percent

fifty percent

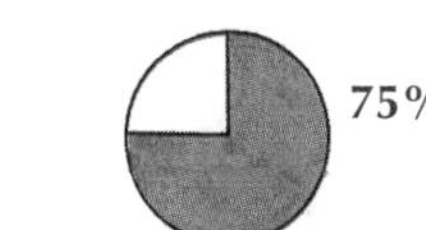

seventy-five percent

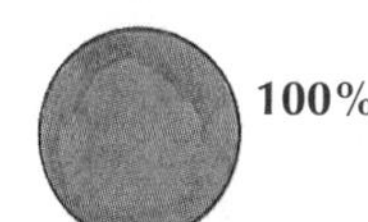

one hundred percent

A. How did you do on the test?
B. I got ________ percent of the answers right.

A. What's the weather forecast?
B. There's a ________ percent chance of rain.

Research and discuss:
What percentage of the people in your country live in cities? live on farms? work in factories? vote in national elections?

TIME
시간

two o'clock

two fifteen/
a quarter after *two*

two thirty/
half past *two*

two forty-five
a quarter to *three*

two oh five

two twenty/
twenty after *two*

two forty/
twenty to *three*

two fifty-five
five to *three*

A. What time is it?
B. It's .

A. What time does the movie begin?
B. At .

two a.m.

two p.m.

noon/
twelve noon

midnight/
twelve midnight

A. When does the train leave?
B. At ________.

A. What time will we arrive?
B. At ________.

Tell about your daily schedule:
What do you do? When?
(I get up at ________. I ....)

Do you usually have enough time to do things, or do you run out of time? Explain.

If there were 25 hours in a day, what would you do with the extra hour? Why?

Tell about the use of time in different cultures or countries you are familiar with:
Do people arrive on time for work? appointments? parties?
Do trains and buses operate exactly on schedule?
Do movies and sports events begin on time?
Do workplaces use time clocks or timesheets to record employees' work hours?

달력

1999 JANUARY 1999						
SUN	MON	TUE	WED	THUR	FRI	SAT
					1	2
3	4	5	6	7	8	9
10	11	12	13	14	15	16
17	18	19	20	21	22	23
24/31	25	26	27	28	29	30

연도 **1. year**

일천구백 구십구년 nineteen ninety-nine

월 **2. month**

일월 January
이월 February
삼월 March
사월 April
오월 May
유월 June
칠월 July
팔월 August
구월 September
시월 October
십일월 November
십이월 December

요일 **3. day**

일요일 Sunday
월요일 Monday
화요일 Tuesday
수요일 Wednesday
목요일 Thursday
금요일 Friday
토요일 Saturday

날짜 **4. date**

일천구백 구십구년 일월 이 일 January 2, 1999
1/2/99
January second, nineteen ninety-nine

A. What year is it?
B. It's ______.

A. What month is it?
B. It's ______.

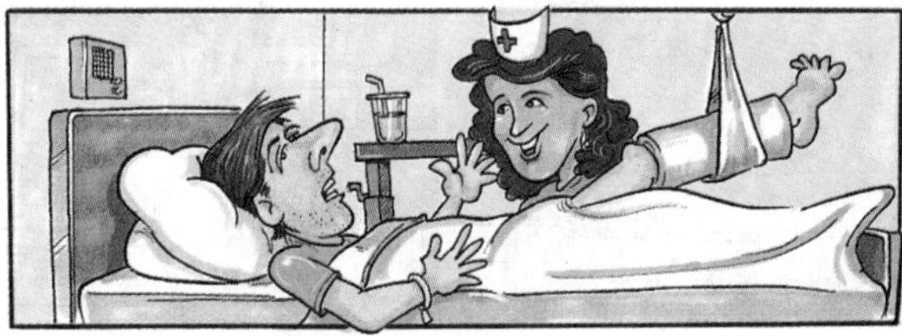

A. What day is it?
B. It's ______.

A. What's today's date?
B. Today is ______.

When did you begin to study English?
What days of the week do you study English? (I study English on ______.)

When is your birthday? (My birthday is on ______.)
What are your favorite months of the year? Why?
What are your least favorite months of the year? Why?

PLACES AROUND TOWN I

도심지 I

A. Where are you going?
B. I'm going to the **appliance store**.

가전제품 판매점 **1.** appliance store
자동차 판매점 **2.** auto dealer/car dealer
제과점 **3.** bakery
은행 **4.** bank
이발소 **5.** barber shop
서점 / 책방 **6.** book store
버스 정류장 **7.** bus station
카페테리아 / 셀프서비스식 식당 **8.** cafeteria
놀이방 / 탁아소 **9.** child-care center/day-care center
세탁소 **10.** cleaners/dry cleaners
도넛 가게 **11.** donut shop
의원 / 병원 **12.** clinic
옷가게 **13.** clothing store
커피숍 **14.** coffee shop
컴퓨터 판매점 **15.** computer store

콘서트 홀 / 연주회장	**16.**	concert hall
편의점	**17.**	convenience store
복사집	**18.**	copy center
델리 / 샌드위치 가게	**19.**	delicatessen/deli
백화점	**20.**	department store
할인매장	**21.**	discount store
약국	**22.**	drug store/pharmacy
꽃집 / 화원	**23.**	flower shop/florist
가구점	**24.**	furniture store
주유소	**25.**	gas station/ service station
식품점	**26.**	grocery store
미용실 / 미장원	**27.**	hair salon
철물점	**28.**	hardware store
헬스클럽	**29.**	health club/spa
병원	**30.**	hospital

A. Hi! How are you today?
B. Fine. Where are you going?
A. To the ________. How about you?
B. I'm going to the ________.

A. Oh, no! I can't find my wallet/purse!
B. Did you leave it at the ________?
A. Maybe I did.

Which of these places are in your neighborhood?
(In my neighborhood there's a/an …………)

도심지 II

A. Where's the **hotel**?
B. It's right over there.

호텔	**1.** hotel	박물관	**9.** museum
아이스크림 가게	**2.** ice cream shop	레코드 가게	**10.** music store
귀금속점	**3.** jewelry store	나이트클럽 / 디스코장	**11.** night club
빨래방	**4.** laundromat	공원	**12.** park
도서관	**5.** library	옥내 주차장 / 차고	**13.** (parking) garage
임산복 전문점	**6.** maternity shop	주차장	**14.** parking lot
모텔	**7.** motel	애완동물 가게	**15.** pet shop
극장	**8.** movie theater		

카메라점 **16.** photo shop
피자 전문점 **17.** pizza shop
우체국 **18.** post office
식당 **19.** restaurant
학교 **20.** school
구두가게 **21.** shoe store
쇼핑센타 **22.** (shopping) mall
슈퍼마켓 **23.** supermarket

극장 **24.** theater
장난감 가게 / 완구점 **25.** toy store
기차역 **26.** train station
여행사 **27.** travel agency
비디오 가게 **28.** video store
안경점 **29.** vision center/eyeglass store
동물원 **30.** zoo

A. Is there a/an ________ nearby?
B. Yes. There's a/an ________ around the corner.

A. Excuse me. Where's the ________?
B. It's down the street, next to the ________.
A. Thank you.

Which of these places are in your neighborhood?
(In my neighborhood there's a/an ....)

THE CITY
도시

A. Where's the ________?
B. On/In/Next to/Between/Across from/
In front of/Behind/Under/Over the ________.

쓰레기통	**1.** trash container	맨홀	**11.** manhole
경찰서	**2.** police station	버스 정류장	**12.** bus stop
교도소	**3.** jail	택시	**13.** taxi/cab/taxicab
법원	**4.** courthouse	택시 운전기사	**14.** taxi driver/cab driver
벤치	**5.** bench	버스	**15.** bus
가로등	**6.** street light	버스 운전기사	**16.** bus driver
아이스크림 트럭	**7.** ice cream truck	주차 미터기	**17.** parking meter
보도	**8.** sidewalk	주차 미터기 담당원	**18.** meter maid
(보도의) 연석	**9.** curb	지하철	**19.** subway
도로	**10.** street	지하철 역	**20.** subway station

전봇대 **21.** utility pole
택시 승강장 **22.** taxi stand
공중전화 박스 **23.** phone booth
공중전화 **24.** public telephone
하수구 **25.** sewer
도로표지판 **26.** street sign
소방서 **27.** fire station
사무용 빌딩 **28.** office building
드라이브 스루 윈도우 **29.** drive-through window
화재 경보기함 **30.** fire alarm box
교차로 **31.** intersection
경찰관 **32.** police officer
횡단보도 **33.** crosswalk
보행자 **34.** pedestrian
교통 신호등 **35.** traffic light/traffic signal
쓰레기 수거차 **36.** garbage truck
신문 가판대 **37.** newsstand
행상인 **38.** street vendor

[An Election Speech]
If I am elected mayor, I'll take care of all the problems we have in our city. We need to do something about our ________s. We also need to do something about our ________s. And look at our ________s! We REALLY need to do something about THEM! We need a new mayor who can solve these problems. If I am elected mayor, we'll be proud of our ________s, ________s, and ________s again! Vote for me!

Step outside. Look around. Describe everything you see.

DESCRIBING PEOPLE AND THINGS
사람 및 사물 묘사

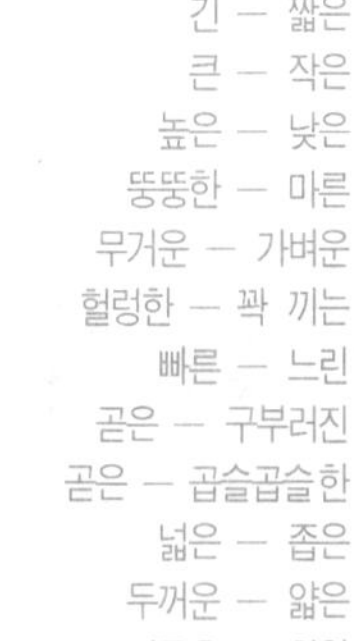

키가 큰 – 키가 작은	**1–2**	tall – short
긴 – 짧은	**3–4**	long – short
큰 – 작은	**5–6**	large/big – small/little
높은 – 낮은	**7–8**	high – low
뚱뚱한 – 마른	**9–10**	heavy/fat – thin/skinny
무거운 – 가벼운	**11–12**	heavy – light
헐렁한 – 꽉 끼는	**13–14**	loose – tight
빠른 – 느린	**15–16**	fast – slow
곧은 – 구부러진	**17–18**	straight – crooked
곧은 – 곱슬곱슬한	**19–20**	straight – curly
넓은 – 좁은	**21–22**	wide – narrow
두꺼운 – 얇은	**23–24**	thick – thin
어두운 – 환한	**25–26**	dark – light
새로운 – 낡은	**27–28**	new – old
어린 / 젊은 – 늙은	**29–30**	young – old
좋은 – 나쁜	**31–32**	good – bad
뜨거운 – 차가운	**33–34**	hot – cold
부드러운 – 딱딱한	**35–36**	soft – hard
쉬운 – 어려운	**37–38**	easy – difficult/hard
부드러운 – 거친	**39–40**	smooth – rough
정돈된 – 어지럽혀진	**41–42**	neat – messy
깨끗한 – 더러운	**43–44**	clean – dirty
시끄러운 – 조용한	**45–46**	noisy/loud – quiet
기혼의 – 미혼의	**47–48**	married – single
부유한 – 가난한	**49–50**	rich/wealthy – poor

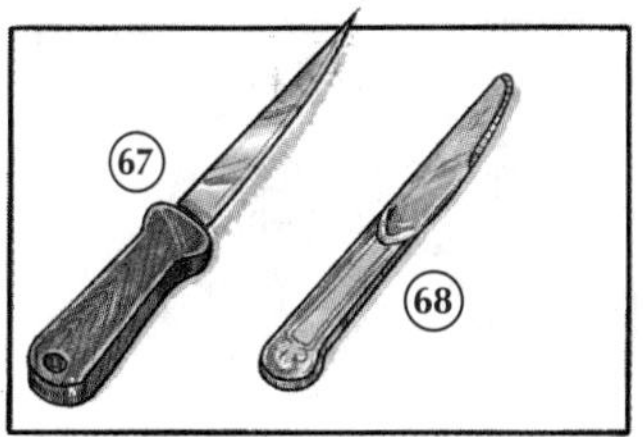

예쁜 / 아름다운 — 못생긴 **51–52** pretty/beautiful – ugly
잘생긴 — 못생긴 **53–54** handsome – ugly
젖은 — 마른 **55–56** wet – dry
열린 — 닫힌 **57–58** open – closed
가득찬 — 빈 **59–60** full – empty

비싼 — 싼 **61–62** expensive – cheap/inexpensive
화려한 — 평범한 **63–64** fancy – plain
빛나는 — (색이) 흐린 **65–66** shiny – dull
날카로운 — 무딘 **67–68** sharp – dull

[1–2]
A. Is your sister **tall**?
B. No. She's **short**.

1–2 Is your sister ________?
3–4 Is his hair ________?
5–6 Is their dog ________?
7–8 Is the bridge ________?
9–10 Is your friend ________?
11–12 Is the box ________?
13–14 Are the pants ________?
15–16 Is the train ________?
17–18 Is the path ________?
19–20 Is his hair ________?
21–22 Is that street ________?
23–24 Is the line ________?
25–26 Is the room ________?
27–28 Is your car ________?
29–30 Is he ________?
31–32 Are your neighbor's children ________?
33–34 Is the water ________?
35–36 Is your pillow ________?
37–38 Is today's homework ________?
39–40 Is your skin ________?
41–42 Is your desk ________?
43–44 Are the dishes ________?
45–46 Is your neighbor ________?
47–48 Is your sister ________?
49–50 Is your uncle ________?
51–52 Is the witch ________?
53–54 Is the pirate ________?
55–56 Are the clothes ________?
57–58 Is the door ________?
59–60 Is the pitcher ________?
61–62 Is that restaurant ________?
63–64 Is the dress ________?
65–66 Is your kitchen floor ________?
67–68 Is the knife ________?

A. Tell me about your ....
B. He's/She's/It's/They're ________.

A. Is your .... ________?
B. No, not at all. As a matter of fact, he's/she's/it's/they're ________.

Describe yourself.
Describe a person you know.
Describe one of your favorite places.

건강상태 및 감정 묘사

A. You look **tired**.
B. I am. I'm VERY **tired**.

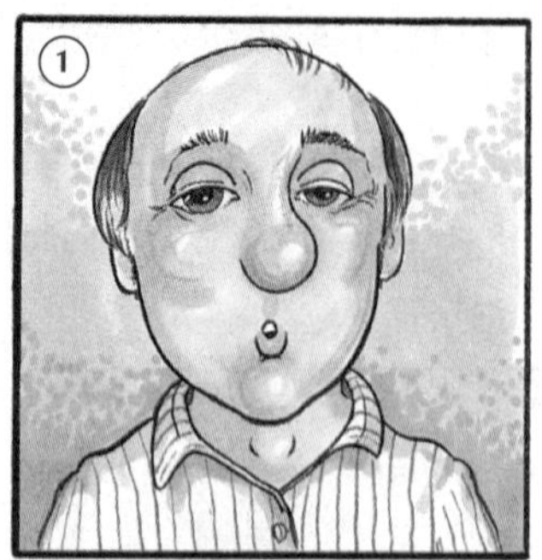

피곤한	**1.** tired	아픈 / 병이 난	**9.** sick/ill
졸린	**2.** sleepy	행복한	**10.** happy
지친	**3.** exhausted	황홀한	**11.** ecstatic
더운	**4.** hot	슬픈 / 불행한	**12.** sad/unhappy
추운	**5.** cold	비참한	**13.** miserable
배고픈	**6.** hungry	만족한	**14.** pleased
목마른	**7.** thirsty	실망한	**15.** disappointed
배부른	**8.** full	기분이 상한	**16.** upset

짜증난 **17.** annoyed
좌절된 **18.** frustrated
성난 / 화난 **19.** angry/mad
분노하는 **20.** furious
혐오스러운 / 구역질나는 **21.** disgusted
놀란 **22.** surprised
충격을 받은 **23.** shocked
초조한 **24.** nervous

걱정스러운 **25.** worried
겁먹은 / 두려운 **26.** scared/afraid
지루한 **27.** bored
자랑스러운 **28.** proud
당황한 **29.** embarrassed
창피한 **30.** ashamed
질투하는 **31.** jealous
혼동된 **32.** confused

A. Are you ________?
B. No. Why do you ask? Do I LOOK ________?
A. Yes. You do.

A. I'm ________.
B. Why?
A. …………

What makes you happy? sad? mad?
When do you feel nervous? annoyed?
Do you ever feel embarrassed? When?

FRUITS

과일

[1–22]
A. This **apple** is delicious! Where did you get it?
B. At *Shaw's Supermarket.*

[23–31]
A. These **grapes** are delicious! Where did you get them?
B. At *Farmer Fred's Fruit Stand.*

사과	**1.** apple	코코넛	**12.** coconut	귤	**22.** tangerine
복숭아	**2.** peach	아보카도	**13.** avocado	포도	**23.** grapes
배	**3.** pear	머스크 멜론	**14.** cantaloupe	버찌	**24.** cherries
바나나	**4.** banana	멜론	**15.** honeydew (melon)	말린 자두	**25.** prunes
자두	**5.** plum	파인애플	**16.** pineapple	대추야자	**26.** dates
살구	**6.** apricot	수박	**17.** watermelon	건포도	**27.** raisins
천도 복숭아	**7.** nectarine	자몽	**18.** grapefruit	블루베리	**28.** blueberries
키위	**8.** kiwi	레몬	**19.** lemon	크렌베리	**29.** cranberries
파파야	**9.** papaya	라임	**20.** lime	나무딸기 / 라스베리	**30.** raspberries
망고	**10.** mango	오렌지	**21.** orange	딸기	**31.** strawberries
무화과 열매	**11.** fig				

A. I'm hungry. Do we have any fruit?
B. Yes. We have ________s* and ________s.*

*With 14–18, use:
We have ________ and ________.

A. Do we have any more ________s?†
B. No. I'll get some more when I go to the supermarket.

†With 14–18, use:
Do we have any more ________?

What are your most favorite fruits?
What are your least favorite fruits?
Which of these fruits grow where you live?
Name and describe other fruits you are familiar with.

야채

A. What do we need from the supermarket?
B. We need **lettuce*** and **peas**.†

*1–12 †13–36

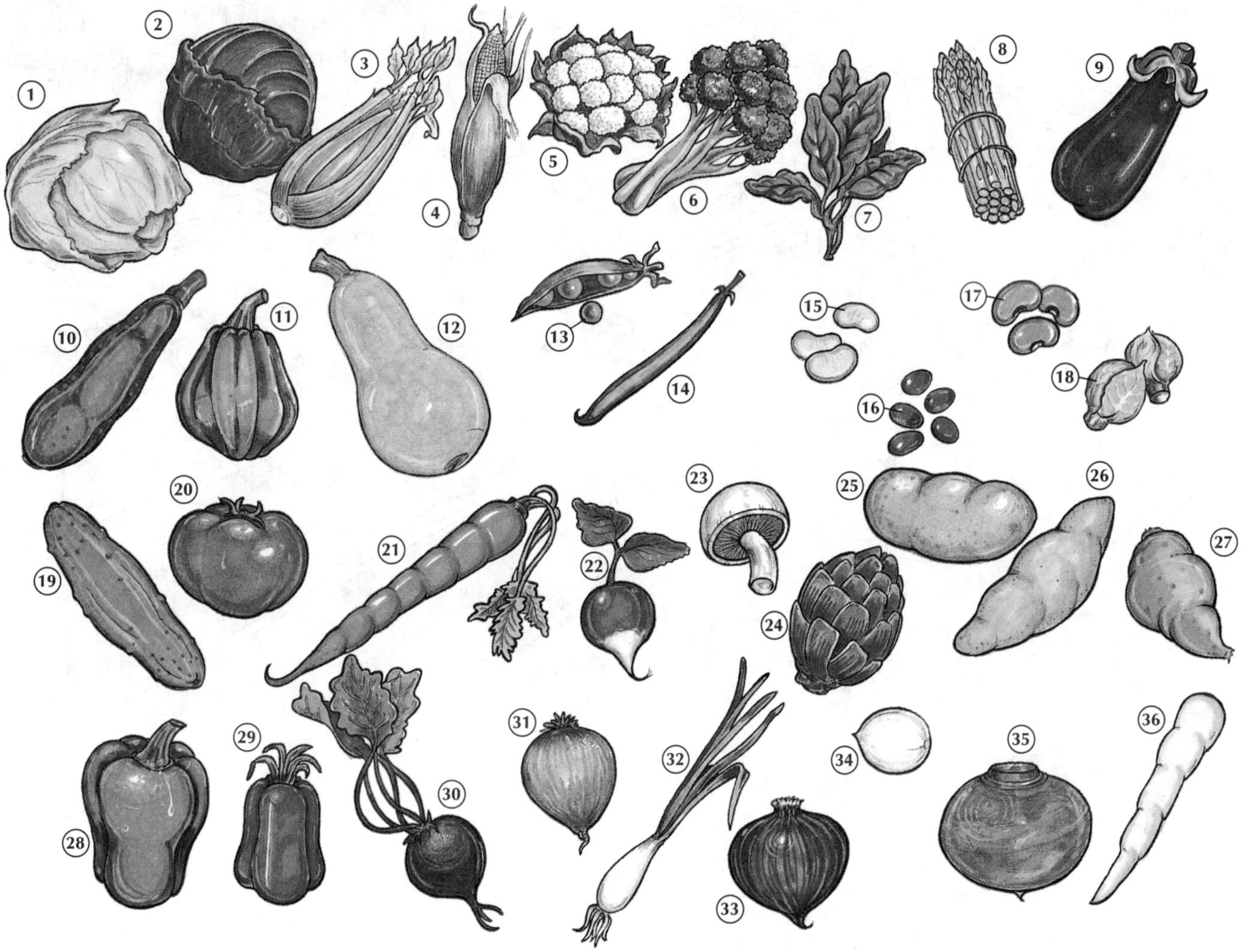

양상추	**1.**	lettuce
양배추	**2.**	cabbage
샐러리	**3.**	celery
옥수수	**4.**	corn
컬리플라워	**5.**	cauliflower
브로콜리	**6.**	broccoli
시금치	**7.**	spinach
아스파라거스	**8.**	asparagus
가지	**9.**	eggplant
애호박	**10.**	zucchini (squash)
도토리호박 / 에이콘 스쿼시	**11.**	acorn squash
버터너트 스쿼시	**12.**	butternut squash
완두콩	**13.**	pea
깍지콩	**14.**	string bean/ green bean
리마콩	**15.**	lima bean
검정콩	**16.**	black bean
강낭콩	**17.**	kidney bean
브러셀스 순	**18.**	brussels sprout
오이	**19.**	cucumber
토마토	**20.**	tomato
당근	**21.**	carrot
무	**22.**	radish
버섯	**23.**	mushroom
아티초크	**24.**	artichoke
감자	**25.**	potato
고구마	**26.**	sweet potato
얌	**27.**	yam
피망	**28.**	green pepper
고추	**29.**	red pepper
비트	**30.**	beet
양파	**31.**	onion
파	**32.**	scallion/ green onion
붉은 양파	**33.**	red onion
진주 양파	**34.**	pearl onion
순무	**35.**	turnip
파스닙 / 사탕당근	**36.**	parsnip

A. How do you like the [1–12] / [13–36]s?
B. It's/They're delicious.

A. *Johnny?* Finish your vegetables!
B. But you KNOW I hate [1–12] / [13–36]s!
A. I know. But it's/they're good for you!

Which vegetables do you like?
Which vegetables don't you like?
Which of these vegetables grow where you live?
Name and describe other vegetables you are familiar with.

THE SUPERMARKET I
슈퍼마켓 I

A. I'm going to the supermarket to get **milk** and **soup**.*
Do we need anything else?

B. Yes. We also need **cereal** and **soda**.*

**With 43, 44, 46, 49, and 55, use: a _____.*

유제품 A. Dairy Products
- 우유 **1.** milk
- 저지방 우유 **2.** low-fat milk
- 탈지유 **3.** skim milk
- 쵸코렛 우유 **4.** chocolate milk
- 버터 밀크 **5.** buttermilk
- 오렌지 쥬스 **6.** orange juice†
- 치즈 **7.** cheese
- 버터 **8.** butter
- 마가린 **9.** margarine
- 사우어 크림 **10.** sour cream
- 크림치즈 **11.** cream cheese
- 코티지 치즈 **12.** cottage cheese
- 요구르트 / 유산균발효유 **13.** yogurt
- 계란 / 달걀 **14.** eggs

통조림류 B. Canned Goods
- 수프 **15.** soup
- 참치 **16.** tuna fish
- 야채 통조림 **17.** (canned) vegetables
- 과일 통조림 **18.** (canned) fruit

포장제품류 C. Packaged Goods
- 시리얼 **19.** cereal
- 과자 **20.** cookies
- 크랙커 **21.** crackers
- 스파게티 **22.** spaghetti
- 국수 **23.** noodles
- 마카로니 **24.** macaroni
- 쌀 **25.** rice

주스류 D. Juice
- 사과 주스 **26.** apple juice
- 파인애플 주스 **27.** pineapple juice
- 자몽 주스 **28.** grapefruit juice
- 토마토 주스 **29.** tomato juice
- 과일 펀치 **30.** fruit punch
- 포도 주스 **31.** grape juice
- 크랜베리 주스 **32.** cranberry juice
- 주스 팩 **33.** juice paks
- 분말 주스 **34.** powdered drink mix

음료수류 E. Beverages
- 소다 / 탄산음료 **35.** soda
- 다이어트 소다 / 무설탕 탄산음료 **36.** diet soda
- 생수 **37.** bottled water

† Orange juice is not a dairy product, but is usually found in this section.

가금류 **F. Poultry**

- 닭고기 **38.** chicken
- 닭다리 **39.** chicken legs
- 드럼스틱 / 닭다리 **40.** drumsticks
- 닭 가슴살 **41.** chicken breasts
- 닭 날개 **42.** chicken wings
- 칠면조 고기 **43.** turkey
- 오리고기 **44.** duck

육류 **G. Meat**

- 소고기다짐 / 다진소고기 **45.** ground beef
- 구이용 고기 **46.** roast
- 스테이크용 고기 **47.** steak
- 국거리용 고기 **48.** stewing meat
- 양다리 **49.** leg of lamb
- 램찹 **50.** lamb chops
- 돼지고기 **51.** pork
- 돼지고기 토막 / 포크 찹 **52.** pork chops
- 갈비 **53.** ribs
- 소시지 **54.** sausages
- 햄 **55.** ham
- 베이컨 **56.** bacon

해물류 / 해산물 **H. Seafood**

어류 / 생선 FISH

- 연어 **57.** salmon
- 넙치 **58.** halibut
- 가자미 / 도다리 **59.** flounder
- 황새치 **60.** swordfish
- 대구 **61.** haddock
- 송어 **62.** trout

어패류 SHELLFISH

- 굴 **63.** oysters
- 가리비 / 스캘롭 **64.** scallops
- 새우 **65.** shrimp
- 홍합 **66.** mussels
- 대합 **67.** clams
- 게 **68.** crabs
- 바닷가재 **69.** lobster

제과류 **I. Baked Goods**

- 잉글리쉬 머핀 **70.** English muffins
- 케이크 **71.** cake
- 피타 빵 **72.** pita bread
- 롤 빵 **73.** rolls
- 식빵 **74.** bread

냉동식품류 **J. Frozen Foods**

- 아이스크림 **75.** ice cream
- 냉동야채 **76.** frozen vegetables
- 냉동요리 **77.** frozen dinners
- 냉동 레모네이드 **78.** frozen lemonade
- 냉동 오렌지주스 **79.** frozen orange juice

A. Excuse me. Where can I find [1–79] ?
B. In the [A–J] Section, next to the [1–79] .
A. Thank you.

A. Pardon me. I'm looking for [1–79] .
B. It's/They're in the [A–J] Section, between the [1–79] and the [1–79] .
A. Thanks.

Which of these foods do you like?
Which foods are good for you?
What brands of these foods do you buy?

THE SUPERMARKET II
슈퍼마켓 II

[1–70]

A. Look! ________ is/are on sale this week!

B. Let's get some!

조제 식품류 / 델리 — A. Deli

- 로스트 비프 **1.** roast beef
- 볼로냐 소시지 **2.** bologna
- 살라미 소시지 **3.** salami
- 햄 **4.** ham
- 칠면조 고기 **5.** turkey
- 콘 비프 **6.** corned beef
- 아메리칸 치즈 **7.** American cheese
- 스위스 치즈 **8.** Swiss cheese
- 프로볼로네 치즈 **9.** provolone
- 모짜렐라 치즈 **10.** mozzarella
- 체다 치즈 **11.** cheddar cheese
- 감자 샐러드 **12.** potato salad
- 콜슬로 / 양배추 샐러드 **13.** cole slaw
- 마카로니 샐러드 **14.** macaroni salad
- 해물 샐러드 **15.** seafood salad

간식류 / 스넥류 — B. Snack Foods

- 감자칩 **16.** potato chips
- 옥수수칩 **17.** corn chips
- 토르티야칩 **18.** tortilla chips
- 나초 칩 **19.** nacho chips
- 프렛즐 **20.** pretzels
- 팝콘 **21.** popcorn
- 견과류 **22.** nuts
- 땅콩 **23.** peanuts

향신료 — C. Condiments

- 케첩 **24.** ketchup
- 겨자 **25.** mustard
- 렐리쉬 **26.** relish
- 오이지 / (오이) 피클 **27.** pickles
- 올리브 **28.** olives
- 소금 **29.** salt
- 후추 **30.** pepper
- 양념 / 향신료 **31.** spices
- 간장 **32.** soy sauce
- 마요네즈 **33.** mayonnaise
- 식용유 **34.** (cooking) oil
- 올리브유 **35.** olive oil
- 식초 **36.** vinegar
- 샐러드 드레싱 **37.** salad dressing

커피와 차 — D. Coffee and Tea

- 커피 **38.** coffee
- 무카페인 커피 **39.** decaffeinated coffee/ decaf coffee
- 홍차 **40.** tea
- 허브티 / 건강차 **41.** herbal tea
- 코코아 **42.** cocoa/ hot chocolate mix

제과용품 — E. Baking Products

- 밀가루 **43.** flour
- 설탕 **44.** sugar
- 케이크 가루 **45.** cake mix

잼과 젤리 **F. Jams and Jellies**
잼 **46.** jam
젤리 **47.** jelly
마멀레이드 **48.** marmalade
땅콩버터 **49.** peanut butter

제지류 **G. Paper Products**
티슈 / 휴지 **50.** tissues
냅킨 **51.** napkins
두루마리 화장지 **52.** toilet paper
종이컵 **53.** paper cups
종이접시 **54.** paper plates
빨대 **55.** straws
종이 타올 **56.** paper towels

가정용품 **H. Household Items**
샌드위치 백 **57.** sandwich bags
쓰레기 봉투 **58.** trash bags
비누 **59.** soap
액체 비누 / 물비누 **60.** liquid soap
은박지 **61.** aluminum foil
비닐 랩 **62.** plastic wrap
파라핀 종이 / 납지 **63.** waxed paper

유아용품 **I. Baby Products**
아기용 씨리얼 **64.** baby cereal
분유 **65.** formula
이유식 **66.** baby food
물휴지 **67.** wipes
(일회용)기저귀 **68.** (disposable) diapers

애완동물 먹이 **J. Pet Food**
애완고양이 먹이 **69.** cat food
애완견 먹이 **70.** dog food

계산대 **K. Checkout Area**
통로 **71.** aisle
쇼핑 카트 **72.** shopping cart
손님 / 고객 **73.** shopper/customer
계산대 **74.** checkout counter
물품 자동이동기 **75.** conveyor belt
쿠폰 / 할인권 **76.** coupons
바코드 판독기 **77.** scanner
계량기 **78.** scale
현금출납기 **79.** cash register
계산원 **80.** cashier
비닐 봉지 **81.** plastic bag
종이 봉지 **82.** paper bag
물건 담아 주는 사람 **83.** bagger/packer
신속 계산대 **84.** express checkout (line)
타블로이드판신문 **85.** tabloid (newspaper)
잡지 **86.** magazine
껌 **87.** (chewing) gum
사탕 **88.** candy
장바구니 **89.** shopping basket

A. Do we need __[1–70]__?
B. No, but we need __[1–70]__.

A. We forgot to get __[1–70]__!
B. I'll get it/them.
Where is it?/Where are they?
A. In the __[A–J]__ Section over there.

Make a complete shopping list of everything you need from the supermarket.
Describe the differences between U.S. supermarkets and food stores in your country.

CONTAINERS AND QUANTITIES

용기와 수량

A. Would you please get a **bag** of *flour* when you go to the supermarket?
B. A **bag** of *flour?* Sure. I'd be happy to.

A. Would you please get two **head**s of *lettuce* when you go to the supermarket?
B. Two **head**s of *lettuce?* Sure. I'd be happy to.

봉지	**1.** bag	다발 / 송이	**5.** bunch	다스 / 열두개	**9.** dozen*
개	**2.** bar	캔 / (깡) 통	**6.** can	개	**10.** ear
병	**3.** bottle	카톤 팩 / 팩	**7.** carton	포기	**11.** head
상자	**4.** box	통	**8.** container	병	**12.** jar

* "a dozen eggs," NOT "a dozen of eggs."

덩어리	**13.** loaf–loaves
통	**14.** pack
봉지	**15.** package
두루마리 / 롤	**16.** roll
여섯개 들이 팩	**17.** six-pack
개	**18.** stick
통	**19.** tub
파인트	**20.** pint
쿼트	**21.** quart
반 갤런	**22.** half-gallon
갤런	**23.** gallon
리터	**24.** liter
파운드	**25.** pound

[At home]

A. What did you get at the supermarket?

B. I got ________, ________, and ________.

[In a supermarket]

A. Is this checkout counter open?

B. Yes, but this is the express line. Do you have more than eight items?

B. No. I only have ________, ________, and ________.

Open your kitchen cabinets and refrigerator. Make a list of all the things you find.

What do you do with empty bottles, jars, and cans? Do you recycle them, reuse them, or throw them away?

계량단위

티스푼
teaspoon
tsp.

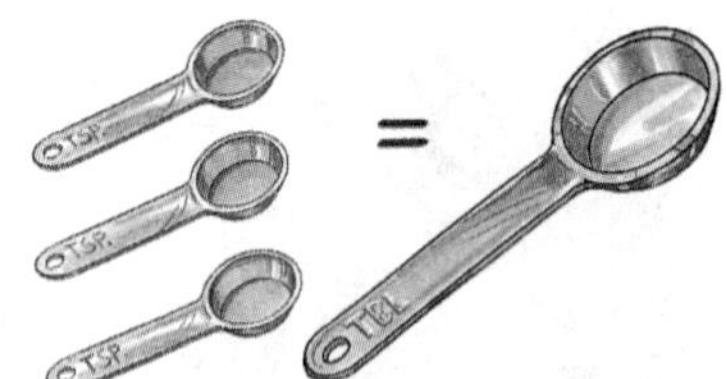

테이블 스푼
tablespoon
Tbsp.

1 온스
1 (fluid) ounce
1 fl. oz.

컵 (8 온스)
cup
8 fl. ozs.

파인트 (16 온스)
pint
pt.
16 fl. ozs.

쿼트 (32 온스)
quart
qt.
32 fl. ozs.

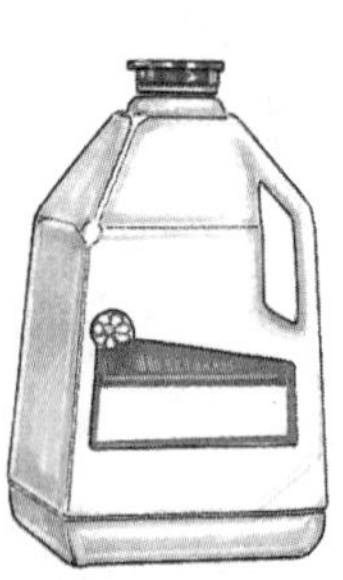

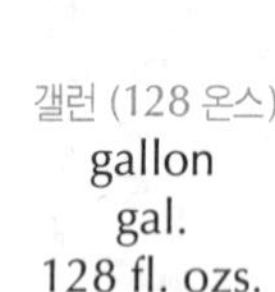

갤런 (128 온스)
gallon
gal.
128 fl. ozs.

A. How much water should I put in?
B. The recipe says to add one ________ of water.

A. This fruit punch is delicious! What's in it?
B. Two ________s of orange juice, three ________s of grape juice, and a ________ of apple juice.

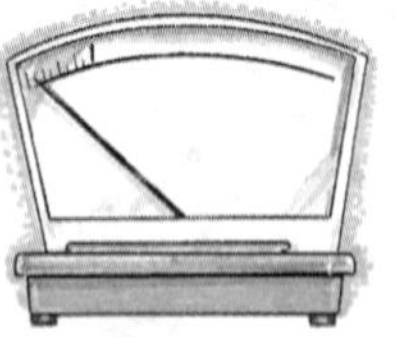

1 온스

an ounce
oz.

¼ 파운드
(4 온스)

a quarter of a pound
¼ lb.
4 ozs.

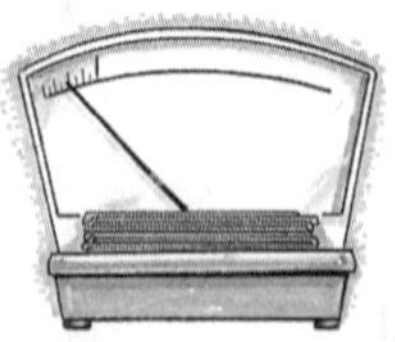

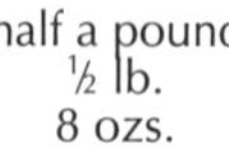

½ 파운드
(8 온스)

half a pound
½ lb.
8 ozs.

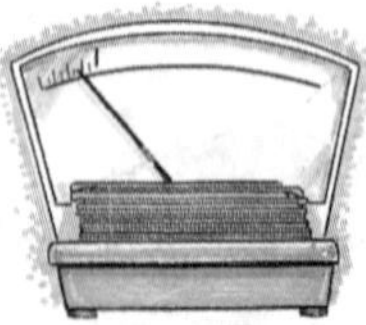

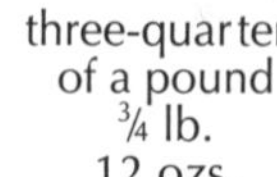

¾ 파운드
(12 온스)

three-quarters of a pound
¾ lb.
12 ozs.

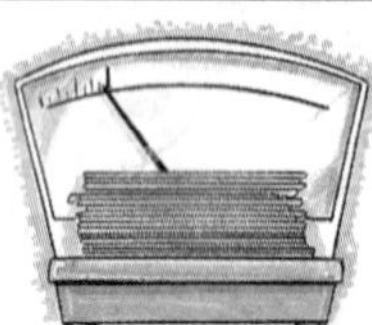

1 파운드
(16 온스)

a pound
lb.
16 ozs.

A. How much roast beef would you like?
B. I'd like ________, please.

A. This chili tastes very good! What did you put in it?
B. ________ of ground beef, ________ of beans, ________ of tomatoes, and ________ of chili powder.

FOOD PREPARATION AND RECIPES

음식준비와 조리법

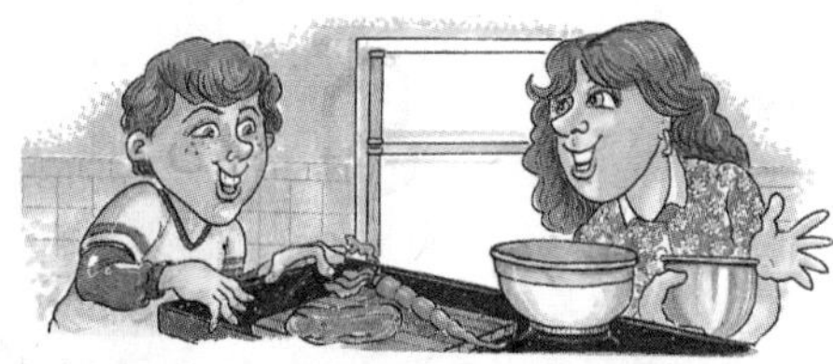

A. Can I help?
B. Yes. Please **cut up** the *vegetables*.

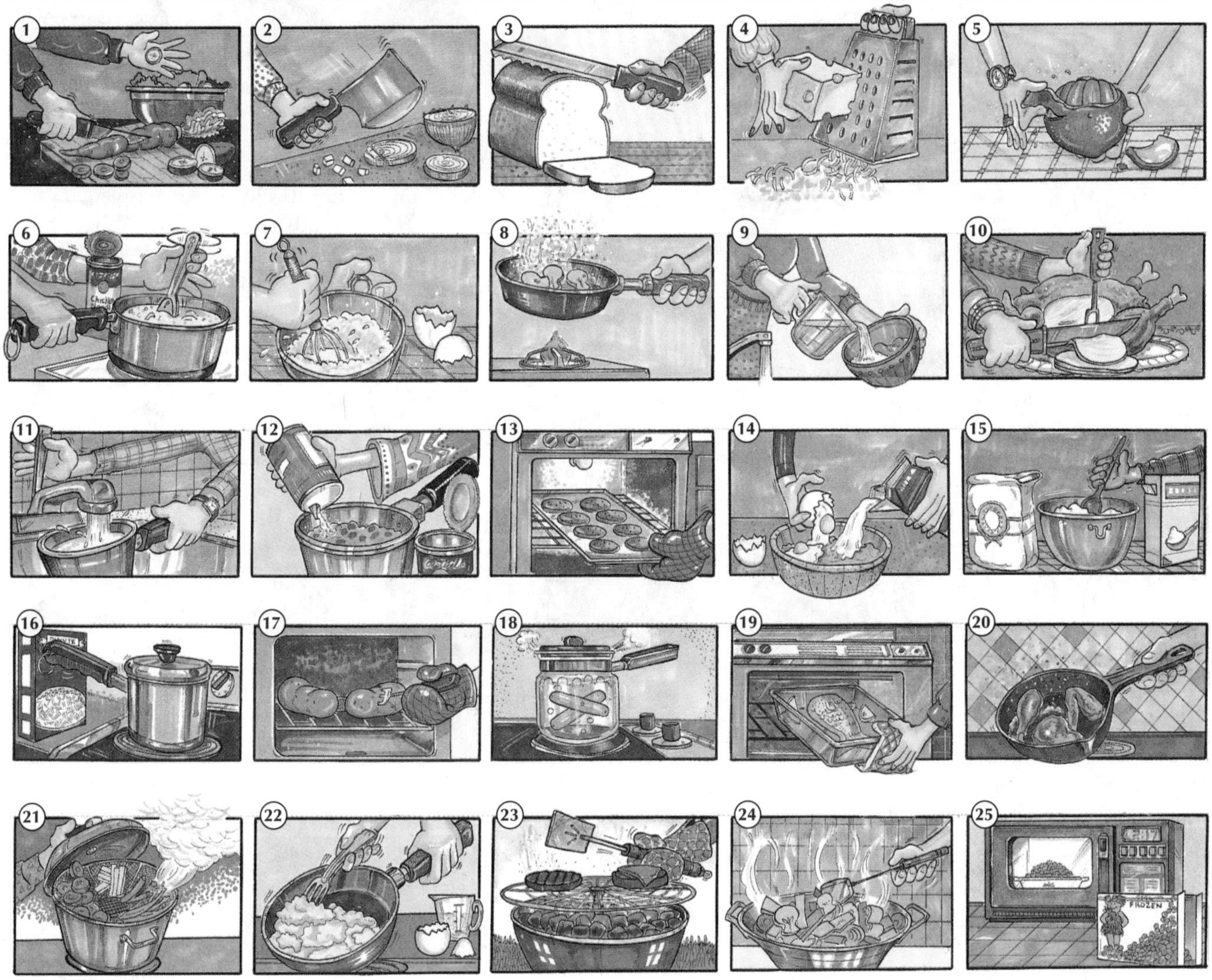

자르다	**1.**	cut (up)
다지다	**2.**	chop (up)
얇게 썰다	**3.**	slice
갈다	**4.**	grate
벗기다	**5.**	peel
젓다	**6.**	stir
휘젓다	**7.**	beat
기름에 볶다	**8.**	saute
붓다	**9.**	pour
얇게 썰다	**10.**	carve
___ 를 ___ 로 채우다	**11.**	fill _____ with _____
___ 에 ___ 을 첨가하다	**12.**	add _____ to _____
___ 을 ___ 에 넣다	**13.**	put _____ in _____
___ 와 ___ 을 혼합하다	**14.**	combine _____ and _____
___ 와 ___ 을 섞다	**15.**	mix _____ and _____
요리하다	**16.**	cook
(빵 · 과자를) 굽다	**17.**	bake
삶다 / 데치다	**18.**	boil
굽다	**19.**	broil
튀기다	**20.**	fry
찌다	**21.**	steam
뒤섞어 익히다	**22.**	scramble
석쇠에 굽다	**23.**	barbecue/grill
볶다	**24.**	stir-fry
전자레인지로 (기름에) 조리하다	**25.**	microwave

[1–25] A. What are you doing?
B. I'm ________ing the ....

[16–25] A. How long should I ________ the ....?
B. For .... minutes/seconds.

What's your favorite recipe? Give instructions and use the units of measure on page 52. For example:
Mix a cup of flour and two tablespoons of sugar.
Add half a pound of butter.
Bake at 350° (degrees) for twenty minutes.

FAST FOODS AND SANDWICHES
패스트 푸드와 샌드위치

도넛	**1.** donut	코카콜라 / 다이어트 콜라펩시 콜라 / 세븐업 / 사이다 / . . .	**15.** Coke/Diet Coke/ Pepsi/7–Up/...	로스트비프 샌드위치	**26.** roast beef sandwich
머핀	**2.** muffin	레모네이드	**16.** lemonade	콘비프 샌드위치	**27.** corned beef sandwich
베이글	**3.** bagel	커피	**17.** coffee	비엘티 / 베이컨, 양상추, 토마토 샌드위치	**28.** BLT/bacon, lettuce,and tomato sandwich
소형 롤빵 / 번	**4.** bun	무카페인 커피	**18.** decaf coffee	흰빵	**29.** white bread
데니쉬 / 페이스트리	**5.** danish/pastry	홍차	**19.** tea	호밀빵	**30.** rye bread
비스킷	**6.** biscuit	아이스 티 / 냉홍차	**20.** iced tea	통밀빵	**31.** whole wheat bread
크루아상	**7.** croissant	우유	**21.** milk	흑빵	**32.** pumpernickel
햄버거	**8.** hamburger	참치 샌드위치	**22.** tuna fish sandwich	피타빵	**33.** pita bread
치즈버거	**9.** cheeseburger	달걀 샐러드 샌드위치	**23.** egg salad sandwich	롤빵	**34.** a roll
핫도그	**10.** hot dog	치킨 샐러드 샌드위치	**24.** chicken salad sandwich	긴 롤빵 / 바게트빵	**35.** a submarine roll
타코	**11.** taco	햄 치즈 샌드위치	**25.** ham and cheese sandwich		
피자 한 조각	**12.** slice of pizza				
칠리 한 그릇	**13.** bowl of chili				
닭 튀김 일 인분	**14.** order of fried chicken				

A. May I help you?
B. Yes. I'd like a/an [1–14] , please.
A. Anything to drink?
B. Yes. I'll have a small/medium-size/ large/extra-large [15–21] .

A. I'd like a [22–28] on [29–35] , please.
B. What do you want on it?
A. Lettuce/tomato/mayonnaise/mustard/...

식당

전채식 A. Appetizers

프루트컵 / 프루트 칵테일 1. fruit cup/ fruit cocktail
토마토 쥬스 2. tomato juice
새우 칵테일 3. shrimp cocktail
닭날개 4. chicken wings
나초 5. nachos
포테이토 스킨/ 감자껍질요리 6. potato skins

샐러드 B. Salads

야채 샐러드 7. tossed salad/ garden salad
그리스 샐러드 8. Greek salad
시금치 샐러드 9. spinach salad
앤티파스토 10. antipasto
시저 샐러드 11. Caesar salad
샐러드 바 12. salad bar

메인코스 / 앙트레 C. Main Courses/Entrees

미트로프 13. meatloaf
로스트비프 / 프라임 리브 14. roast beef/ prime rib
비프가스/ 비프커트렛 15. veal cutlet
통닭구이 16. baked chicken
생선구이 17. broiled fish
스파게티와 미트 볼 18. spaghetti and meatballs

결들이 요리 D. Side Dishes

통감자구이 19. a baked potato
으깬 감자요리 20. mashed potatoes
프렌치 프라이/감자 튀김 21. french fries
밥 22. rice
국수 23. noodles
모듬야채 24. mixed vegetables

디저트 / 후식 E. Dessert

쵸코렛 케익 25. chocolate cake
애플파이 26. apple pie
아이스크림 27. ice cream
젤로 28. jello
푸딩 29. pudding
아이스크림 선대 30. ice cream sundae

[Ordering dinner]

A. May I take your order?
B. Yes, please. For the appetizer I'd like the [1–6].
A. And what kind of salad would you like?
B. I'll have the [7–12].
A. And for the main course?
B. I'd like the [13–18], please.
A. What side dish would you like with that?
B. Hmm. I think I'll have [19–24].

[Ordering dessert]

A. Would you care for some dessert?
B. Yes. I'll have [25–29] /an [30].

Do you go to restaurants? Which ones? What do you order? Describe some popular desserts in your country.

COLORS
색깔

A. What's your favorite color?
B. **Red.**

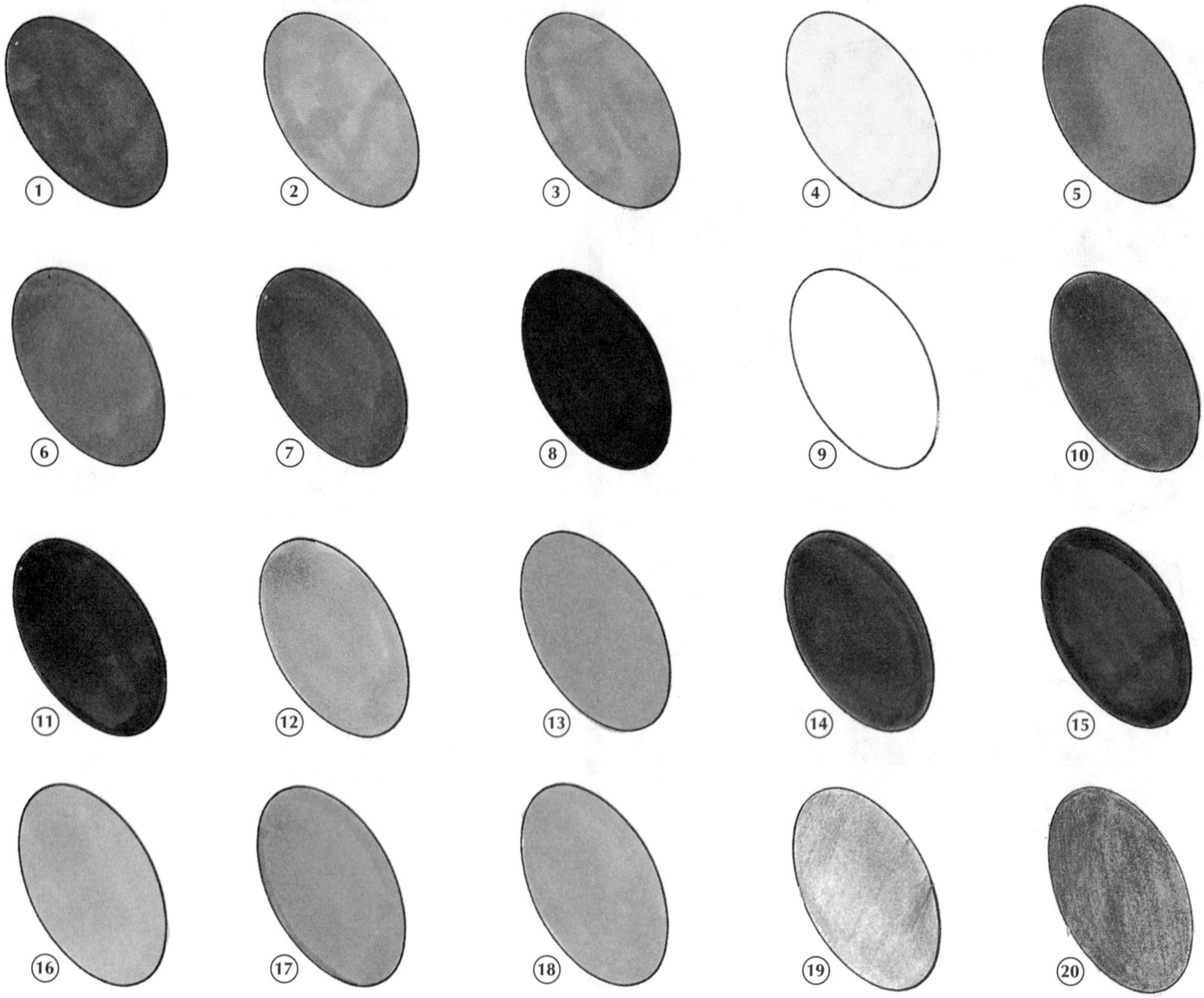

빨강색	**1.** red	검정색	**8.** black	감청색	**15.** navy blue
분홍색	**2.** pink	흰색	**9.** white	청록색	**16.** turquoise
오렌지색	**3.** orange	회색	**10.** gray	꽃분홍	**17.** hot pink
노랑색	**4.** yellow	밤색	**11.** brown	형광 초록색	**18.** neon green
초록색	**5.** green	베이지색	**12.** beige	은색	**19.** silver
파랑색	**6.** blue	연두색	**13.** light green	금색	**20.** gold
보라색	**7.** purple	짙은 초록색	**14.** dark green		

A. I like your _______ shirt.
You look very good in _______.
B. Thank you. _______ is my favorite color.

A. My color TV is broken.
B. What's the matter with it?
A. People's faces are _______, the sky is _______, and the grass is _______!

Do you know the flags of different countries? What are the colors of the flags you know?
What color makes you happy? What color makes you sad? Why?

CLOTHING

의복

A. I think I'll wear my new **shirt** today.
B. Good idea!

셔츠 / 긴팔셔츠 **1.** shirt/long-sleeved shirt
반팔 셔츠 **2.** short-sleeved shirt
드레스 셔츠 / 와이셔츠 **3.** dress shirt
스포츠 셔츠 **4.** sport shirt
폴로 셔츠 / 메리야스 셔츠 / 스포츠 셔츠 **5.** polo shirt/jersey/sport shirt
플란넬 셔츠 **6.** flannel shirt
블라우스 **7.** blouse
터틀넥 **8.** turtleneck
바지 **9.** pants/slacks
청바지 **10.** (blue) jeans

고르덴 바지 **11.** corduroy pants/corduroys
치마 **12.** skirt
원피스 **13.** dress
우주복 **14.** jumpsuit
반바지 **15.** shorts
스웨타 **16.** sweater
브이 — 넥 **17.** V-neck sweater
카디건 **18.** cardigan sweater
멜빵 바지 **19.** overalls
유니폼 / 단체복 **20.** uniform

재킷 / 스포츠재킷 / 스포츠코트 **21.** jacket/sports jacket/sports coat
재킷 **22.** jacket
블레이저 **23.** blazer
정장 **24.** suit
스리피스 / 조끼있는 정장 **25.** three-piece suit
조끼 **26.** vest
넥타이 **27.** tie/necktie
나비 넥타이 **28.** bowtie
턱시도 **29.** tuxedo
이브닝 드레스 / (여성용) 야회복 **30.** (evening) gown

SLEEPWEAR, UNDERWEAR, AND FOOTWEAR
잠옷, 속옷 및 신발류

잠옷 / 파자마	**1.** pajamas	미니 삼각팬티	**11.** (bikini) panties/ underpants	펌프스	**24.** pumps
나이트 가운	**2.** nightgown	삼각팬티	**12.** briefs	단화	**25.** loafers
나이트 셔츠 / 셔츠잠옷	**3.** nightshirt	브래지어	**13.** bra	운동화	**26.** sneakers
목욕가운	**4.** bathrobe/robe	캐미솔	**14.** camisole	테니스화 / 정구화	**27.** tennis shoes
실내화	**5.** slippers	슬립 / 속치마	**15.** slip	조깅화	**28.** running shoes
런닝셔츠 / 티셔츠	**6.** undershirt/ tee shirt	반 속치마	**16.** half slip	농구화	**29.** high tops/ high-top sneakers
삼각팬티	**7.** (jockey) shorts/ underpants	스타킹	**17.** stockings	샌들	**30.** sandals
사각팬티	**8.** boxer shorts	팬티 스타킹	**18.** pantyhose	발가락 샌들	**31.** thongs/flip-flops
팬티형 서포터 / 급소 보호대	**9.** athletic supporter/ jockstrap	타이츠	**19.** tights	부츠	**32.** boots
긴 내의	**10.** long underwear/ long johns	양말	**20.** socks	작업용 장화	**33.** work boots
		무릎 양말 / 목이 긴 양말	**21.** knee socks	등산화	**34.** hiking boots
		구두	**22.** shoes	카우보이 부츠	**35.** cowboy boots
		하이힐	**23.** (high) heels	모카신	**36.** moccasins

[1–21] A. I can't find my new ________.
B. Did you look in the bureau/dresser/closet?
A. Yes, I did.
B. Then it's/they're probably in the wash.

[22–36] A. Are those new ________?
B. Yes, they are.
A. They're very nice.
B. Thanks.

EXERCISE CLOTHING AND OUTERWEAR

운동복과 방한복

티셔츠	1.	tee shirt
탱크탑 / 소매없는 셔츠	2.	tank top
운동복 상의 / 트레닝복 상의	3.	sweatshirt
운동복 하의 / 트레닝복 하의	4.	sweat pants
운동용 반바지	5.	running shorts
테니스 바지	6.	tennis shorts
스판덱스 반바지	7.	lycra shorts
조깅복	8.	jogging suit/ running suit
에어로빅복	9.	leotard
타이츠	10.	tights
머리띠	11.	sweatband
코트	12.	coat
오바 / 오버코트	13.	overcoat
잠바	14.	jacket
스포츠용 잠바	15.	windbreaker
스키 잠바	16.	ski jacket
가죽 잠바	17.	bomber jacket
파카	18.	parka
오리털 잠바	19.	down jacket
오리털 조끼	20.	down vest
우 / 비옷	21.	raincoat
판쵸	22.	poncho
바바리(코트)	23.	trenchcoat
고무신	24.	rubbers
(손가락) 장갑	25.	gloves
벙어리 장갑	26.	mittens
테있는 모자	27.	hat
모자	28.	cap
야구모자	29.	baseball cap
베레모	30.	beret
우비 모자	31.	rain hat
스키 모자	32.	ski hat
스키마스크	33.	ski mask
(보온용) 귀덮개 / 귀마개	34.	ear muffs
목도리	35.	scarf

[1–11]

A. Excuse me. I found this/these ________ in the dryer. Is it/Are they yours?

B. Yes. It's/They're mine. Thank you.

[12–35]

A. What's the weather like today?

B. It's cool/cold/raining/snowing.

A. I think I'll wear my ________.

JEWELRY AND ACCESSORIES

보석 및 악세사리

A. Oh, no! I think I lost my **ring**!
B. I'll help you look for it.

A. Oh, no! I think I lost my **earrings**!
B. I'll help you look for them.

반지	**1.** ring	넥타이 핀	**13.** tie pin/tie tack
약혼반지	**2.** engagement ring	넥타이 크립	**14.** tie clip
결혼반지	**3.** wedding ring/wedding band	벨트 / 혁대	**15.** belt
귀걸이	**4.** earrings	열쇠고리	**16.** key ring/key chain
목걸이	**5.** necklace	지갑	**17.** wallet
진주목걸이	**6.** pearl necklace/pearls	동전지갑	**18.** change purse
체인 / 목걸이 줄	**7.** chain	핸드백 / 손가방	**19.** pocketbook/purse/handbag
구슬 목걸이	**8.** beads	숄더백	**20.** shoulder bag
장식핀	**9.** pin	토트백 / 여성용 큰 손가방	**21.** tote bag
시계 / 손목시계	**10.** watch/wrist watch	책가방	**22.** book bag
팔찌	**11.** bracelet	배낭	**23.** backpack
커프스 단추	**12.** cuff links	서류가방	**24.** briefcase
		우산	**25.** umbrella

[In a store]
A. Excuse me. Is this/Are these _______ on sale this week?
B. Yes. It's/They're half price.

[On the street]
A. Help! Police! Stop that man/woman!
B. What happened?!
A. He/She just stole my _______ and my _______!

Do you like to wear jewelry? What jewelry do you have?
In your country, what do men, women, and children use to carry their things?

DESCRIBING CLOTHING
옷에 관한 표현

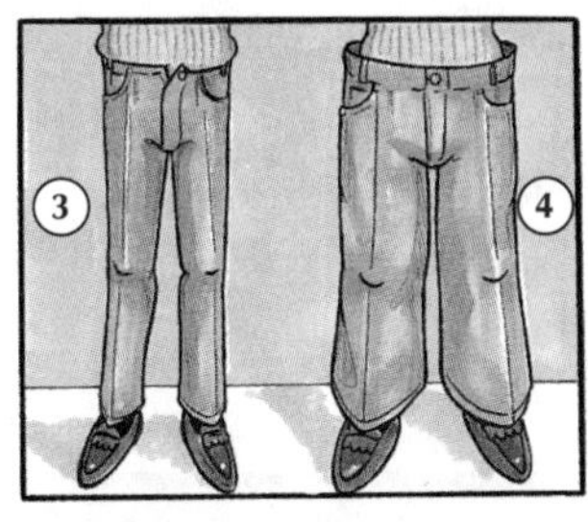

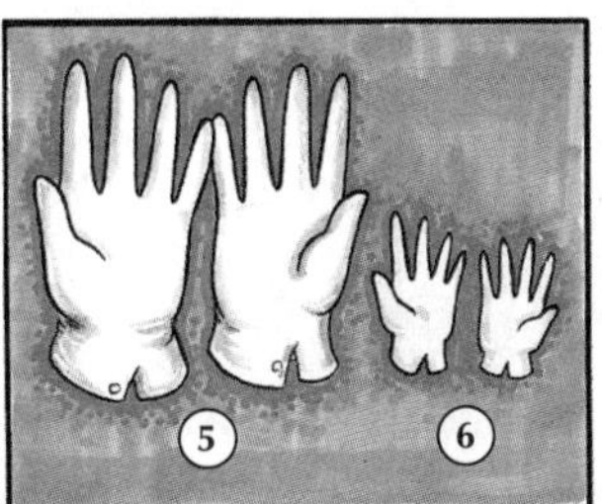

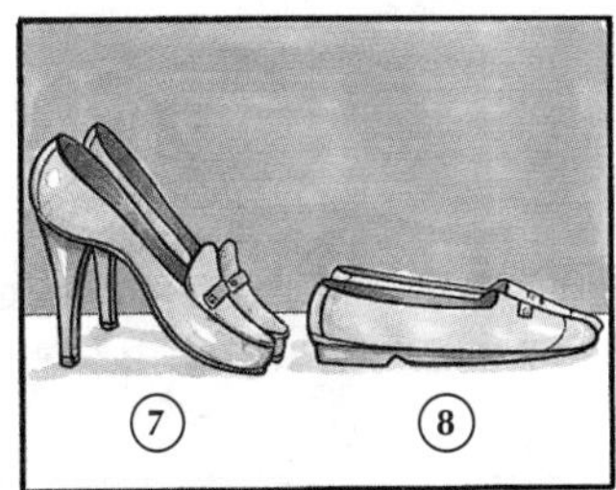

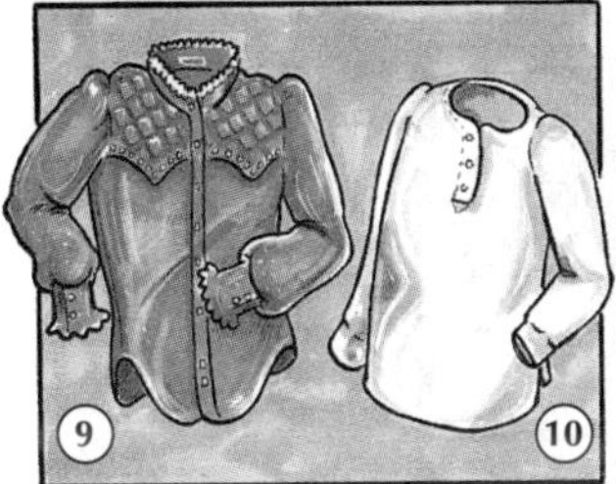

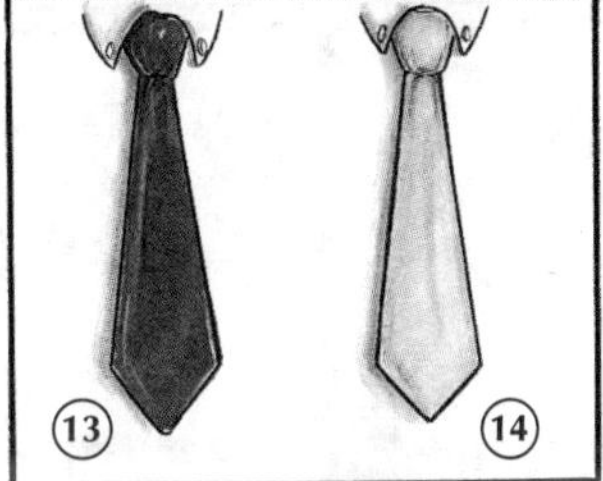

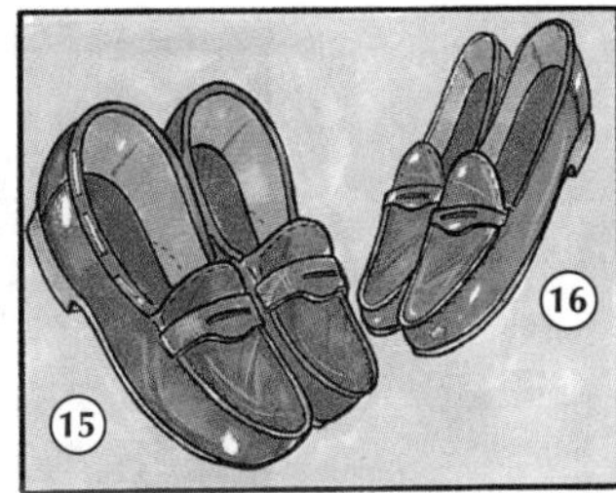

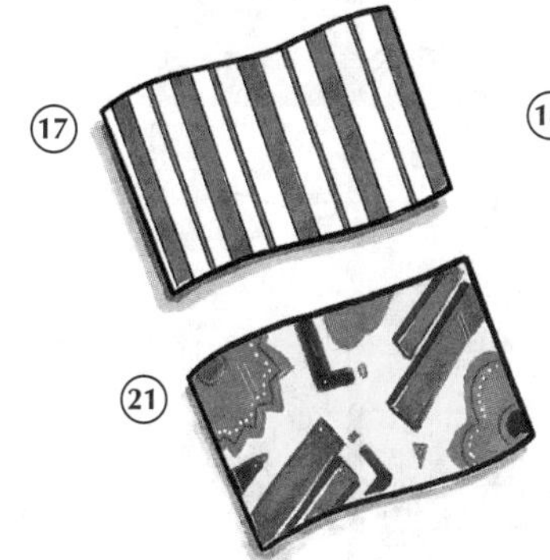

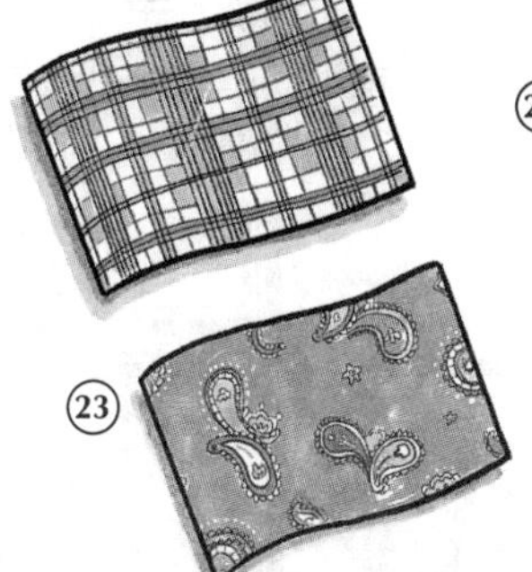

긴 — 짧은	**1–2** long – short		줄무늬의	**17.** striped
꽉 끼는 — 헐렁한	**3–4** tight – loose/baggy		바둑판 무늬의	**18.** checked
큰 — 작은	**5–6** large/big – small		격자무늬의 / 체크무늬의	**19.** plaid
높은 — 낮은	**7–8** high – low		물방울 무늬의	**20.** polka dot
화려한 — 평범한	**9–10** fancy – plain		프린트한 / 날염의	**21.** print
무거운 — 가벼운	**11–12** heavy – light		꽃무늬의	**22.** flowered
진한 — 옅은 / 흐린	**13–14** dark – light		페이즐리 무늬의	**23.** paisley
넓은 — 좁은	**15–16** wide – narrow		단색 파랑	**24.** solid *blue*

[1–2]
A. Are the sleeves too **long**?
B. No. They're too **short**.

1–2 Are the sleeves too _____?
3–4 Are the pants too _____?
5–6 Are the gloves too _____?
7–8 Are the heels too _____?

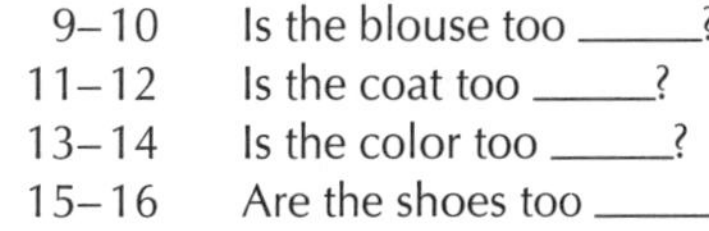

9–10 Is the blouse too _____?
11–12 Is the coat too _____?
13–14 Is the color too _____?
15–16 Are the shoes too _____?

[17–24]
A. How do you like this _____ tie/shirt/skirt?
B. Actually, I prefer that _____ one.

Describe your favorite clothing.

THE DEPARTMENT STORE

백화점

A. Excuse me. Where's the **store directory**?
B. It's over there, next to the **escalator**.

- 안내도 **1.** (store) directory
- 에스컬레이터 **2.** escalator
- 남성의류 코너 **3.** Men's Clothing Department
- 향수코너 **4.** Perfume Counter
- 귀금속코너 **5.** Jewelry Counter
- 엘리베이터 / 승강기 **6.** elevator
- 신사용 화장실 **7.** men's room
- 숙녀용 화장실 **8.** ladies' room
- 식수대 **9.** water fountain
- 옥내 주차장 **10.** parking garage
- 여성의류 코너 **11.** Women's Clothing Department
- 아동의류 코너 **12.** Children's Clothing Department
- 주방기구 코너 **13.** Housewares Department
- 가구코너 **14.** Furniture Department/Home Furnishings Department
- 가전제품 코너 **15.** Household Appliances Department
- 전자제품 코너 **16.** Electronics Department
- 고객 서비스 창구 **17.** Customer Assistance Counter/ Customer Service Counter
- 스넥코너 **18.** snack bar
- 선물포장센타 **19.** Gift Wrap Counter
- (옥외) 주차장 **20.** parking lot
- 물품 인도소 **21.** customer pickup area

A. Pardon me. Is this the way to the ________?
B. Yes, it is./No, it isn't.

A. I'll meet you at/in/near/in front of the ________.
B. Okay. What time?
A. At *3:00*.

Describe a department store you know. Tell what is on each floor.

비디오와 오디오 장비

A. May I help you?
B. Yes, please. I'm looking for a **TV**.

텔레비전	**1.** TV/television set	스테레오	**13.** stereo system/sound system
리모컨	**2.** remote control (unit)	녹음기	**14.** tape recorder
비디오	**3.** VCR/videocassette recorder	소형녹음기 / 워크맨	**15.** (personal) cassette player/ Walkman
(공) 테이프	**4.** (blank) videotape	휴대용 스테레오	**16.** portable stereo system/boom box
비디오 / (비디오) 테이프	**5.** video/(video)tape	(카세트) 테이프	**17.** (audio) tape/(audio) cassette
캠코더 / 비디오 카메라	**6.** camcorder/video camera	시디 / 컴팩트 디스크	**18.** CD/compact disc
턴테이블	**7.** turntable	레코드	**19.** record
테이프 데크	**8.** tape deck	헤드폰	**20.** set of headphones
시디 플레이어	**9.** CD player/compact disc player	라디오	**21.** radio
앰프	**10.** amplifier	단파 라디오	**22.** shortwave radio
튜너	**11.** tuner	시계 라디오	**23.** clock radio
스피커	**12.** speaker		

A. How do you like my ________?
B. It's great/fantastic/awesome!

A. Which company makes a good ________?
B. In my opinion, the best ________ is made by ....

What video and audio equipment do you have or want?
In your opinion, which brands are the best?

COMPUTERS, TELEPHONES, AND CAMERAS
컴퓨터, 전화기 및 카메라

A. Can you recommend a good **computer**?*
B. Yes. This **computer** here is excellent.

**With 9, use:* Can you recommend good ______?

컴퓨터 **1.** computer
모니터 **2.** monitor
디스크 드라이브 **3.** disk drive
키보드 / 자판 **4.** keyboard
마우스 **5.** mouse
프린터 **6.** printer
모뎀 **7.** modem
(플로피) 디스크 / 디스켓 **8.** (floppy) disk/diskette
(컴퓨터) 소프트웨어 **9.** (computer) software
휴대용 컴퓨터 **10.** portable computer
노트북 컴퓨터 **11.** notebook computer
전화기 **12.** telephone/phone
무선전화기 **13.** portable phone/portable telephone
자동응답기 **14.** answering machine
팩스 **15.** fax machine
카메라 **16.** camera
망원렌즈 **17.** zoom lens
카메라 가방 **18.** camera case
플래시 **19.** flash attachment
삼각대 **20.** tripod
필름 **21.** film
환등기 **22.** slide projector
스크린 **23.** (movie) screen
전동타자기 **24.** electric typewriter
전자타자기 **25.** electronic typewriter
(전자) 계산기 **26.** calculator
업소용 계산기 **27.** adding machine
전압조절기 **28.** voltage regulator
어댑터 **29.** adapter

A. Excuse me. Do you sell ______s?†
B. Yes. We carry a complete line of ______s.†

†*With 9 and 21, use the singular.*

A. Which ______ is the best?
B. This one here. It's made by ....

Do you have a camera? What kind is it? What do you take pictures of?
Does anyone you know have an answering machine? When you call, what does the machine say?
How have computers changed the world?

완구점

A. Excuse me. I'm looking for (a/an) ________(s) for my *grandson.**
B. Look in the next aisle.
A. Thank you.

* *grandson/granddaughter/...*

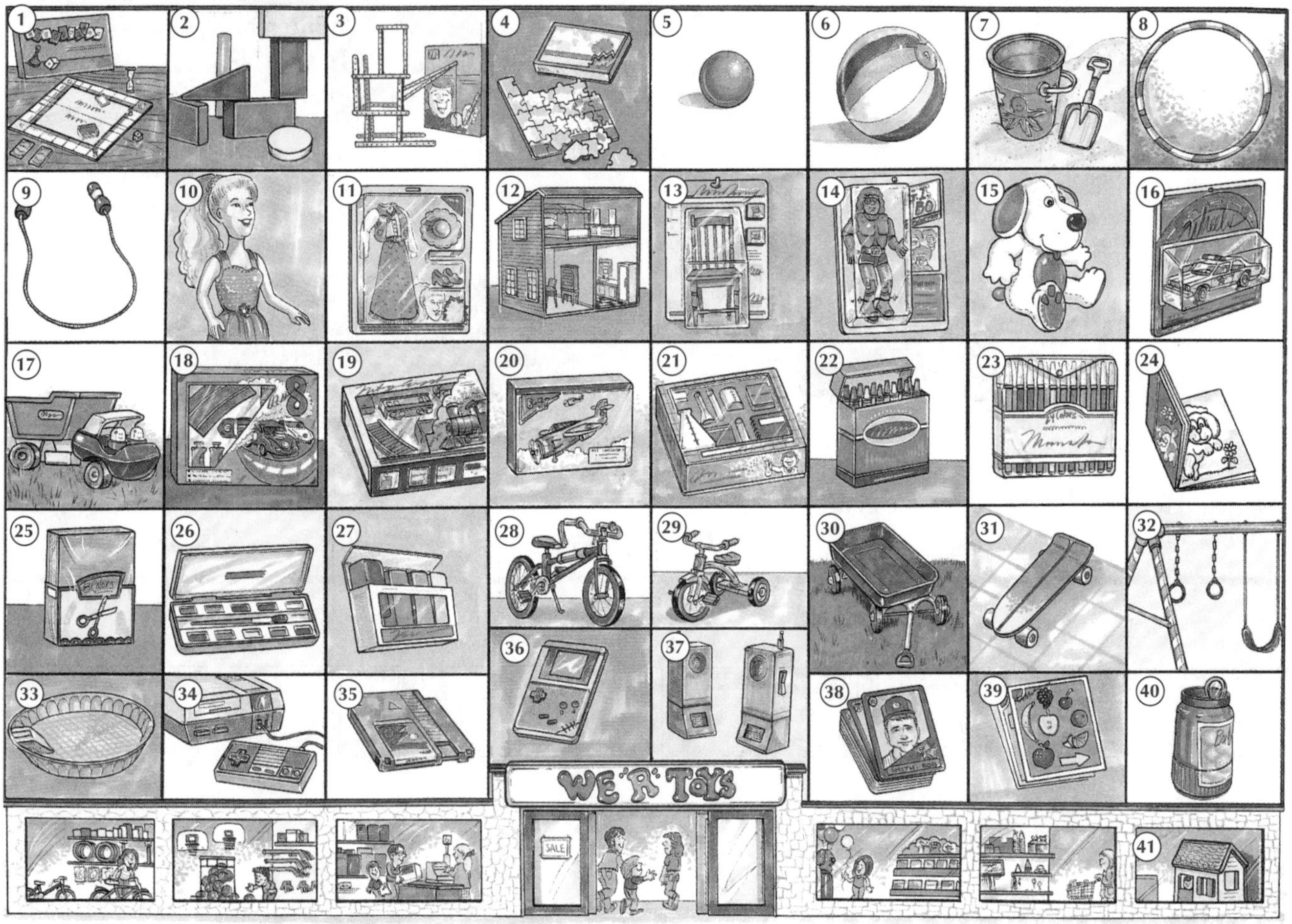

(보드) 게임	**1.**	(board) game
블록	**2.**	(building) blocks
공작세트	**3.**	construction set
퍼즐	**4.**	(jigsaw) puzzle
고무공	**5.**	rubber ball
비치볼	**6.**	beach ball
양동이와 삽	**7.**	pail and shovel
훌라후프	**8.**	hula hoop
줄넘기 줄	**9.**	jump rope
인형	**10.**	doll
인형옷	**11.**	doll clothing
인형집	**12.**	doll house
인형집 가구	**13.**	doll house furniture
소형인형	**14.**	action figure
봉제인형	**15.**	stuffed animal
장난감 차 / 미니카	**16.**	matchbox car
장난감 트럭	**17.**	toy truck
경주용 자동차세트	**18.**	racing car set
기차세트	**19.**	train set
모형조립세트	**20.**	model kit
과학실험세트	**21.**	science kit
크레용	**22.**	crayons
(칼라) 사이펜	**23.**	(color) markers
색칠하기 그림책	**24.**	coloring book
색도화지	**25.**	construction paper
물감세트	**26.**	paint set
점토 / 찰흙	**27.**	(modeling) clay
(두발) 자전거	**28.**	bicycle
(세발) 자전거	**29.**	tricycle
수레	**30.**	wagon
스케이트 보드	**31.**	skateboard
그네세트	**32.**	swing set
물놀이통	**33.**	plastic swimming pool/wading pool
비디오게임기구	**34.**	video game system
(비디오) 게임 팩	**35.**	(video) game cartridge
휴대용 비디오게임기구	**36.**	hand-held video game
워키 토키	**37.**	walkie-talkie (set)
트레이딩 카드	**38.**	trading cards
스티커	**39.**	stickers
비누방울액	**40.**	bubble soap
놀이집	**41.**	play house

A. I don't know what to get my ....-year-old son/daughter for his/her birthday.
B. What about (a) ________?

A. Mom/Dad? Can we buy this/these ________?
B. No, *Johnny*. Not today.

What toys are most popular in your country?
What were your favorite toys when you were a child?

화폐

동전 / Coins

	Name	Value	Written as:	
1.	penny	one cent	1¢	$ .01
2.	nickel	five cents	5¢	$ .05
3.	dime	ten cents	10¢	$ .10
4.	quarter	twenty-five cents	25¢	$ .25
5.	half dollar	fifty cents	50¢	$ .50
6.	silver dollar	one dollar		$1.00

A. How much is a **penny** worth?
B. A penny is worth **one cent**.

A. *Soda* costs *seventy-five cents.*
Do you have enough change?
B. Yes. I have a/two/three _______(s) and . . . .

지폐 / Currency

	Name	We sometimes say:	Value	Written as:
7.	(one-)dollar bill	a one	one dollar	$ 1.00
8.	five-dollar bill	a five	five dollars	$ 5.00
9.	ten-dollar bill	a ten	ten dollars	$ 10.00
10.	twenty-dollar bill	a twenty	twenty dollars	$ 20.00
11.	fifty-dollar bill	a fifty	fifty dollars	$ 50.00
12.	(one-)hundred dollar bill	a hundred	one hundred dollars	$100.00

A. I need to go to the supermarket.
Do you have any cash?
B. Let me see. I have a **twenty-dollar bill**.
A. **Twenty dollars** is enough. Thanks.

A. Can you change a **five-dollar bill/a five**?
B. Yes. I've got ***five* one-dollar bills/*five* ones**.

Written as	*We say:*
$1.20	one dollar and twenty cents a dollar twenty
$2.50	two dollars and fifty cents two fifty
$37.43	thirty-seven dollars and forty-three cents thirty-seven forty-three

How much do you pay for a loaf of bread? a hamburger? a cup of coffee? a gallon of gas?

Name and describe the coins and currency in your country. What are they worth in U.S. dollars?

은행

- 수표책 **1.** checkbook
- 수표장부 **2.** check register
- 월별 거래 내역서 **3.** monthly statement
- 통장 **4.** bank book
- 여행자수표 **5.** traveler's checks
- 크레디트카드 **6.** credit card
- (자동)현금카드 **7.** ATM card
- 입금용지 **8.** deposit slip
- 예금 청구서 / 인출용지 **9.** withdrawal slip
- 수표 **10.** check
- 우편환 **11.** money order
- 대출 신청서 / 융자 신청서 **12.** loan application
- (은행) 금고 **13.** (bank) vault
- 귀중품 보관소 / 대여금고 **14.** safe deposit box
- 은행출납원 **15.** teller
- 경비원 / 청원경찰 **16.** security guard
- 현금 자동 인출기 **17.** automatic teller (machine)/ ATM (machine)
- 은행원 **18.** bank officer

[1–7]

A. What are you looking for?

B. My ________. I can't find it/them anywhere!

[8–12]

A. What are you doing?

B. I'm filling out this ________.

A. For how much?

B. ....

[13–18]

A. How many ________s does the State Street Bank have?

B. ....

Do you have a bank account? What kind? Where?
Do you ever use traveler's checks? When?
Do you have a credit card? What kind? When do you use it?

THE BODY
인체

[1–23, 27–79]
A. My doctor checked my **head** and said everything is okay.
B. I'm glad to hear that.

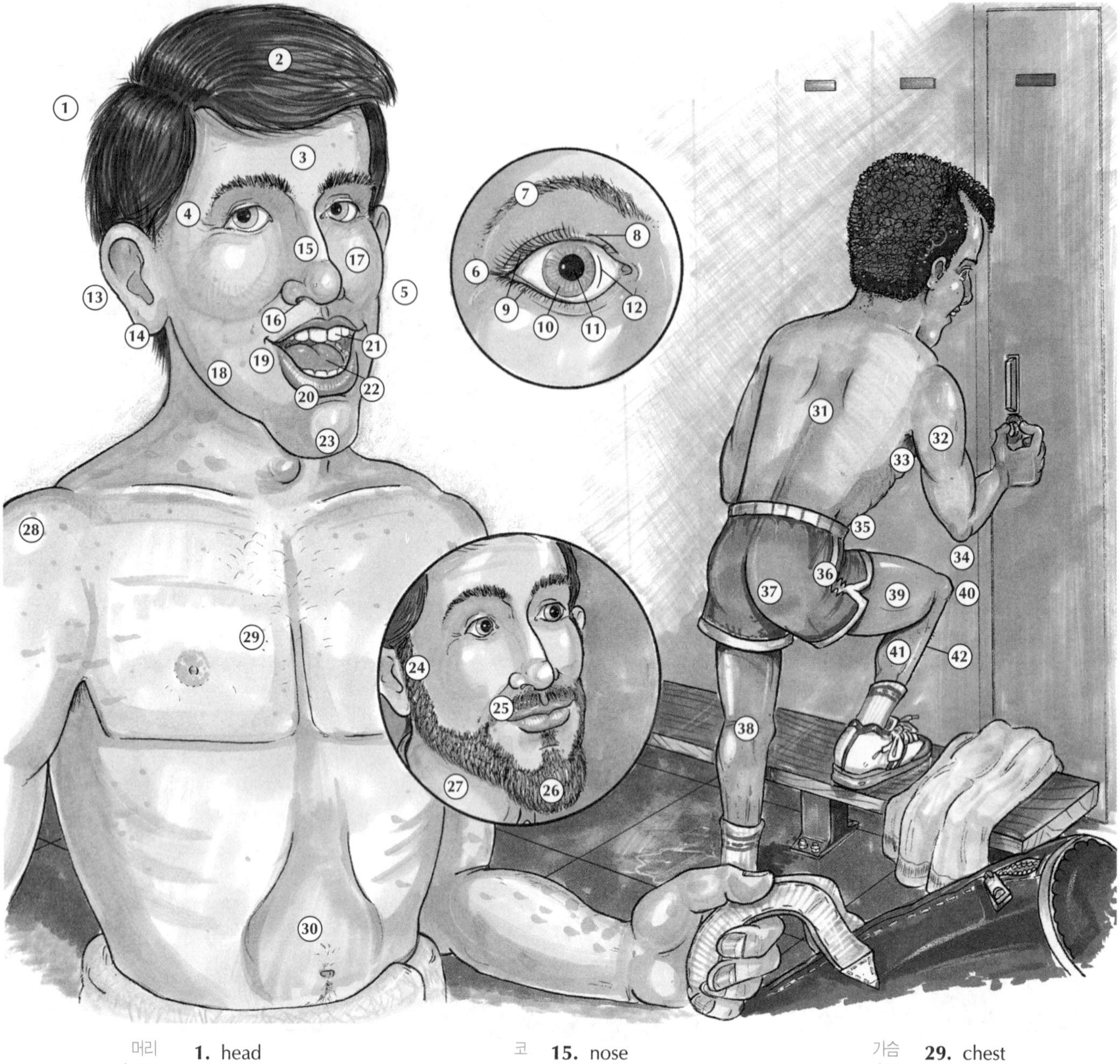

머리	**1.** head	코	**15.** nose	가슴	**29.** chest
머리카락 / 모발	**2.** hair	콧구멍	**16.** nostril	복부 / 배	**30.** abdomen
이마	**3.** forehead	뺨 / 볼	**17.** cheek	등	**31.** back
관자놀이	**4.** temple	턱	**18.** jaw	팔	**32.** arm
얼굴	**5.** face	입	**19.** mouth	겨드랑이	**33.** armpit
눈	**6.** eye	입술	**20.** lip	팔꿈치	**34.** elbow
눈썹	**7.** eyebrow	치아	**21.** tooth–teeth	허리	**35.** waist
눈꺼풀	**8.** eyelid	혀	**22.** tongue	힙 / 골반 / 둔부	**36.** hip
속눈썹	**9.** eyelashes	(아래) 턱 / 턱끝	**23.** chin	엉덩이 / 둔부	**37.** buttocks
홍채	**10.** iris	구레나룻	**24.** sideburn	다리	**38.** leg
눈동자 / 동공	**11.** pupil	콧수염	**25.** mustache	허벅지	**39.** thigh
각막	**12.** cornea	턱수염	**26.** beard	무릎	**40.** knee
귀	**13.** ear	목	**27.** neck	종아리	**41.** calf
귓불	**14.** earlobe	어깨	**28.** shoulder	정강이	**42.** shin

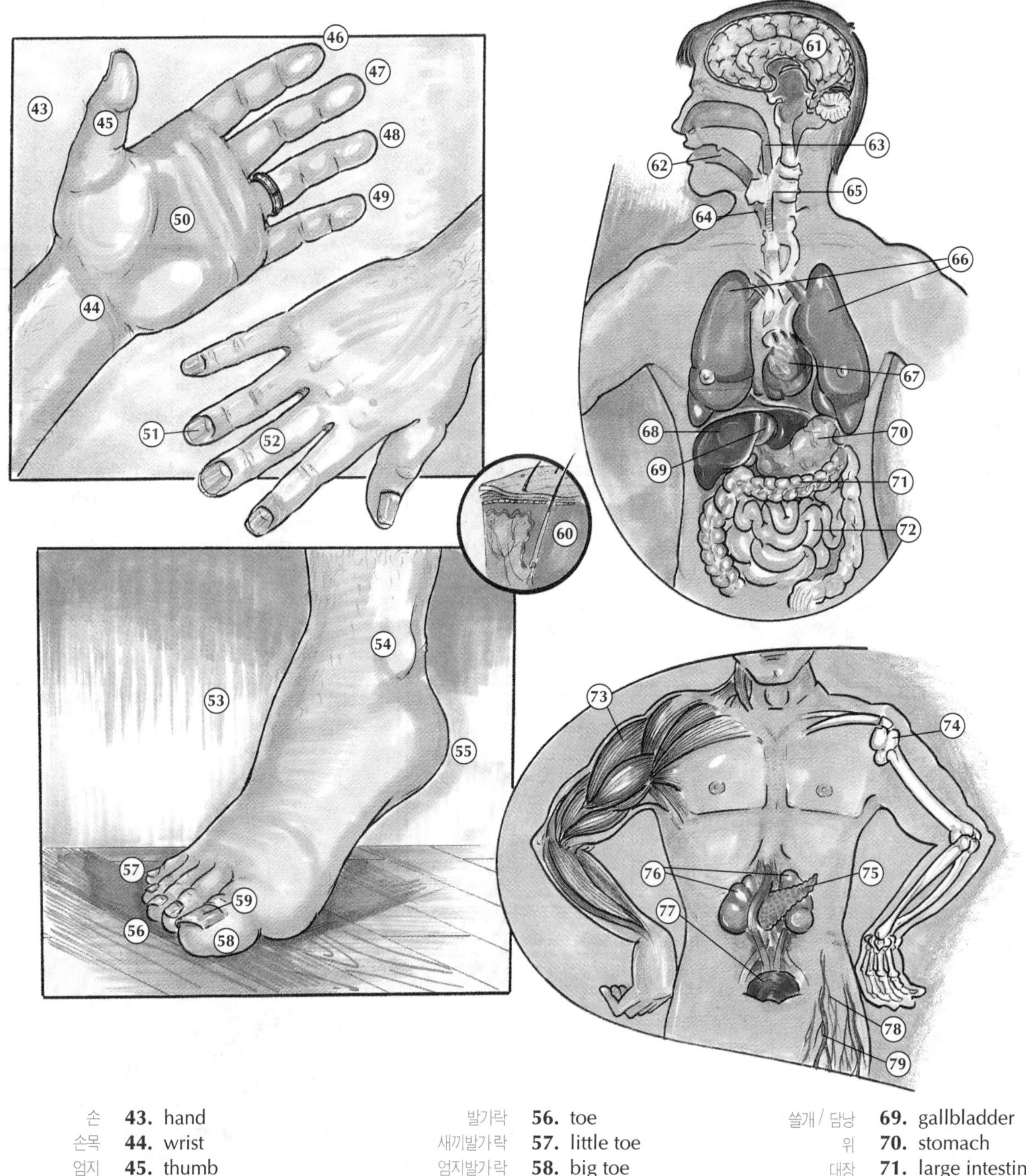

손	**43.** hand	발가락	**56.** toe	쓸개 / 담낭	**69.** gallbladder
손목	**44.** wrist	새끼발가락	**57.** little toe	위	**70.** stomach
엄지	**45.** thumb	엄지발가락	**58.** big toe	대장	**71.** large intestine
집게손가락	**46.** (index) finger	발톱	**59.** toenail	소장	**72.** small intestine
가운뎃손가락	**47.** middle finger	피부	**60.** skin	근육	**73.** muscles
약손가락	**48.** ring finger	뇌	**61.** brain	뼈	**74.** bones
새끼손가락	**49.** pinky/little finger	목(구멍)	**62.** throat	췌장	**75.** pancreas
손바닥	**50.** palm	식도	**63.** esophagus	신장	**76.** kidneys
손톱	**51.** fingernail	기관 / 숨통	**64.** windpipe	방광	**77.** bladder
손가락 관절 / 마디	**52.** knuckle	척추	**65.** spinal cord	정맥	**78.** veins
발	**53.** foot	폐	**66.** lungs	동맥	**79.** arteries
발목	**54.** ankle	심장	**67.** heart		
발꿈치	**55.** heal	간	**68.** liver		

[1, 3–8, 13–23, 27–34, 36–60]
A. Ooh!
B. What's the matter?
A. {My ________ hurts! / My ________s hurt!

[61–79]
A. My doctor wants me to have some tests.
B. Why?
A. She's concerned about my ________.

Describe yourself as completely as you can.
Which parts of the body are most important at school? at work? when you play your favorite sport?

질병, 증세 및 부상

A. What's the matter?
B. I have a/an [1–19] .

A. What's the matter?
B. I have [20–26] .

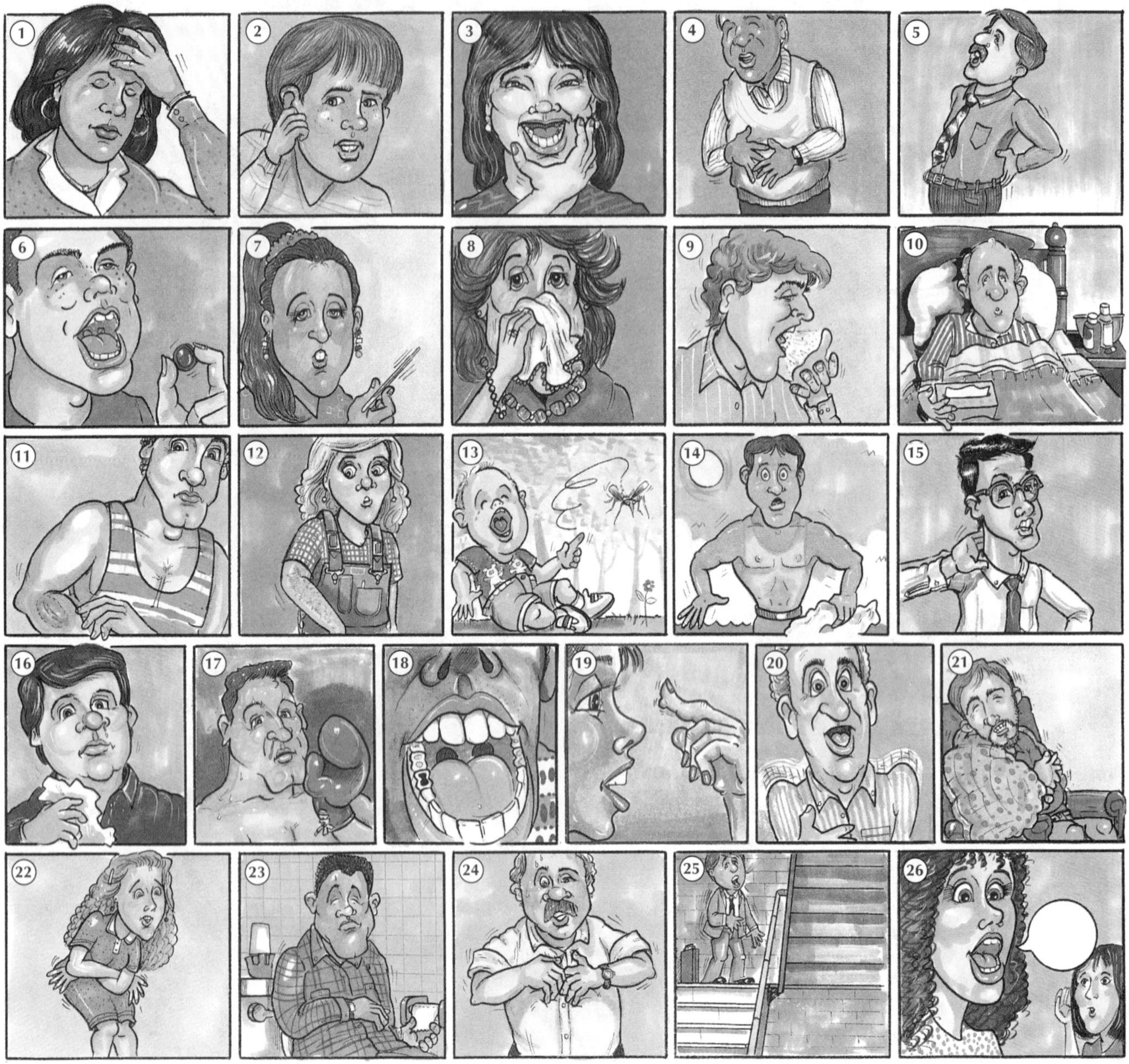

두통	**1.** headache	바이러스	**10.** virus	사마귀	**19.** wart
귀앓이 / 이통	**2.** earache	염증 / 감염	**11.** infection	딸꾹질	**20.** (the) hiccups
치통	**3.** toothache	두드러기 / 발진	**12.** rash	오한	**21.** (the) chills
복통	**4.** stomachache	벌레물린 상처	**13.** insect bite	(근육의) 경련	**22.** cramps
요통	**5.** backache	햇볕에 의한 화상	**14.** sunburn	설사	**23.** diarrhea
인후염	**6.** sore throat	목이 뻐근함	**15.** stiff neck	흉부통	**24.** chest pain
열	**7.** fever/ temperature	콧물	**16.** runny nose	숨이 참	**25.** shortness of breath
감기	**8.** cold	코피	**17.** bloody nose	후두염	**26.** laryngitis
기침	**9.** cough	충치	**18.** cavity		

A. What's the matter?
B. I feel [27–30].
I'm [31–32].
I'm [33–38] ing.

A. What's the matter?
B. I [39–48] ed my ....
My .... is/are [49–50].

기절할 것 같은	**27.** faint	색색거리다	**35.** wheeze	찰과상을 입다	**43.** scrape
어지러운	**28.** dizzy	트림하다	**36.** burp	타박상을 입다	**44.** bruise
메스꺼운	**29.** nauseous	구토하다	**37.** vomit/throw up	화상을 입다	**45.** burn
부은	**30.** bloated	출혈하다	**38.** bleed	골절되다	**46.** break–broke
코가 막힌 / 충혈된	**31.** congested	뒤틀리다	**39.** twist	다치다 —	**47.** hurt–hurt
지친	**32.** exhausted	삐다	**40.** sprain	베다 —	**48.** cut–cut
기침하다	**33.** cough	탈구시키다	**41.** dislocate	부은	**49.** swollen
재채기하다	**34.** sneeze	긁히다	**42.** scratch	가려운	**50.** itchy

A. How do you feel?
B. Not so good./Not very well./Terrible!
A. What's the matter?
B. ...., ..., and ....
A. I'm sorry to hear that.

Tell about the last time you didn't feel well. What was the matter?

Tell about a time you hurt yourself. What happened? How?

What are the symptoms of a cold? a heart problem?

MEDICAL AND DENTAL CARE

의료와 치과치료

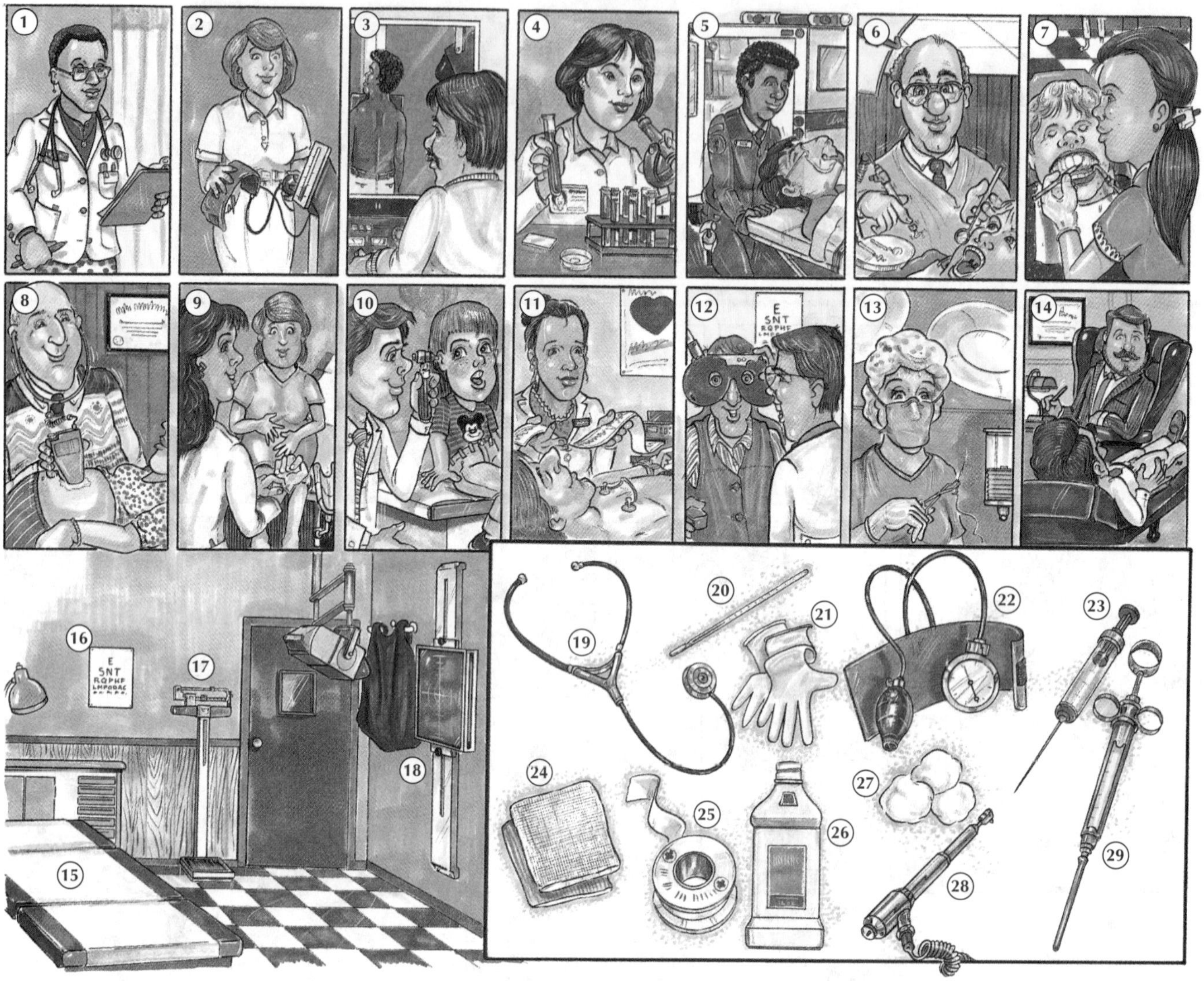

의사 / 내과의사	**1.** doctor/physician	소아과의사	**10.** pediatrician	장갑	**21.** gloves
간호사	**2.** nurse	심장전문의	**11.** cardiologist	혈압측정기	**22.** blood pressure gauge
방사선과 전문의 / 방사선과 기사	**3.** X-ray technician	검안사	**12.** optometrist	주사	**23.** needle/syringe
임상 병리사	**4.** lab technician	외과의사	**13.** surgeon	붕대 / 가제	**24.** bandages/gauze
의무구조원	**5.** EMT/emergency medical technician	정신과의사	**14.** psychiatrist	반창고	**25.** adhesive tape
치과의사	**6.** dentist	진료대	**15.** examination table	알코올	**26.** alcohol
구강 위생사	**7.** (oral) hygienist	시력검사표	**16.** eye chart	탈지면	**27.** cotton balls
산과의사	**8.** obstetrician	체중계	**17.** scale	드릴	**28.** drill
부인과의사	**9.** gynecologist	엑스레이기	**18.** X-ray machine	마취제	**29.** anesthetic/ Novocaine
		청진기	**19.** stethoscope		
		체온계	**20.** thermometer		

[1–14]
A. What do you do?
B. I'm a/an ________.

[15–18]
A. Please step over here to the ________.
B. Okay.

[19–29]
A. Please hand me the ________.
B. Here you are.

Where do you go for medical care? How often? Who examines you? What does he/she do?

치료와 병원

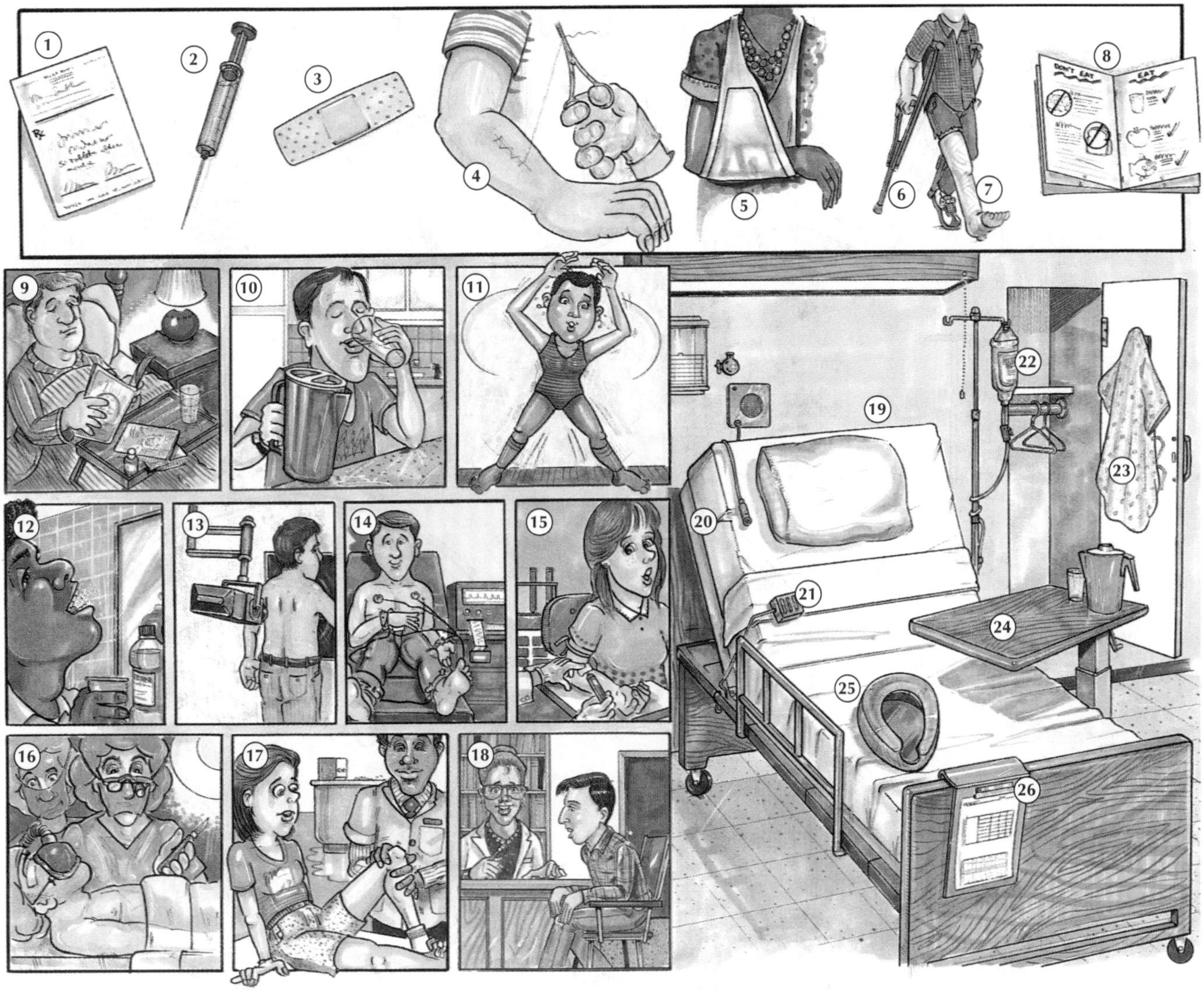

- 처방(전) **1.** prescription
- 주사 **2.** injection/shot
- 일회용 밴드 **3.** bandaid
- 봉합 **4.** stitches
- 삼각끈 **5.** sling
- 목발 **6.** crutches
- 깁스 붕대 **7.** cast
- 식이요법 **8.** diet
- 누워서 휴식하다 **9.** rest in bed
- 수분을 섭취하다 **10.** drink fluids
- 운동하다 **11.** exercise
- 양치질하다 **12.** gargle
- 엑스레이 촬영 **13.** X-rays
- 검사 **14.** tests
- 혈액검사 **15.** blood work/ blood tests
- 수술 **16.** surgery
- 물리치료 **17.** physical therapy
- 상담 **18.** counseling
- 병원침대 **19.** hospital bed
- 호출버튼 **20.** call button
- 침대조절기 **21.** bed control
- 정맥주사 **22.** I.V.
- 환자복 **23.** hospital gown
- 베드 테이블 **24.** bed table
- 환자용 변기 **25.** bed pan
- 진료 차트 **26.** medical chart

[1–8]
A. What did the doctor do?
B. She/He gave me (a/an) ______.

[9–18]
A. What did the doctor say?
B. { She/He told me to [9–12].
She/He told me I need [13–18].

[19–26]
A. This is your ______.
B. I see.

When did you have your last medical checkup?
What did the doctor say?

Have you ever been in the hospital?
When? Why? Tell about your experience.

MEDICINE

의약품

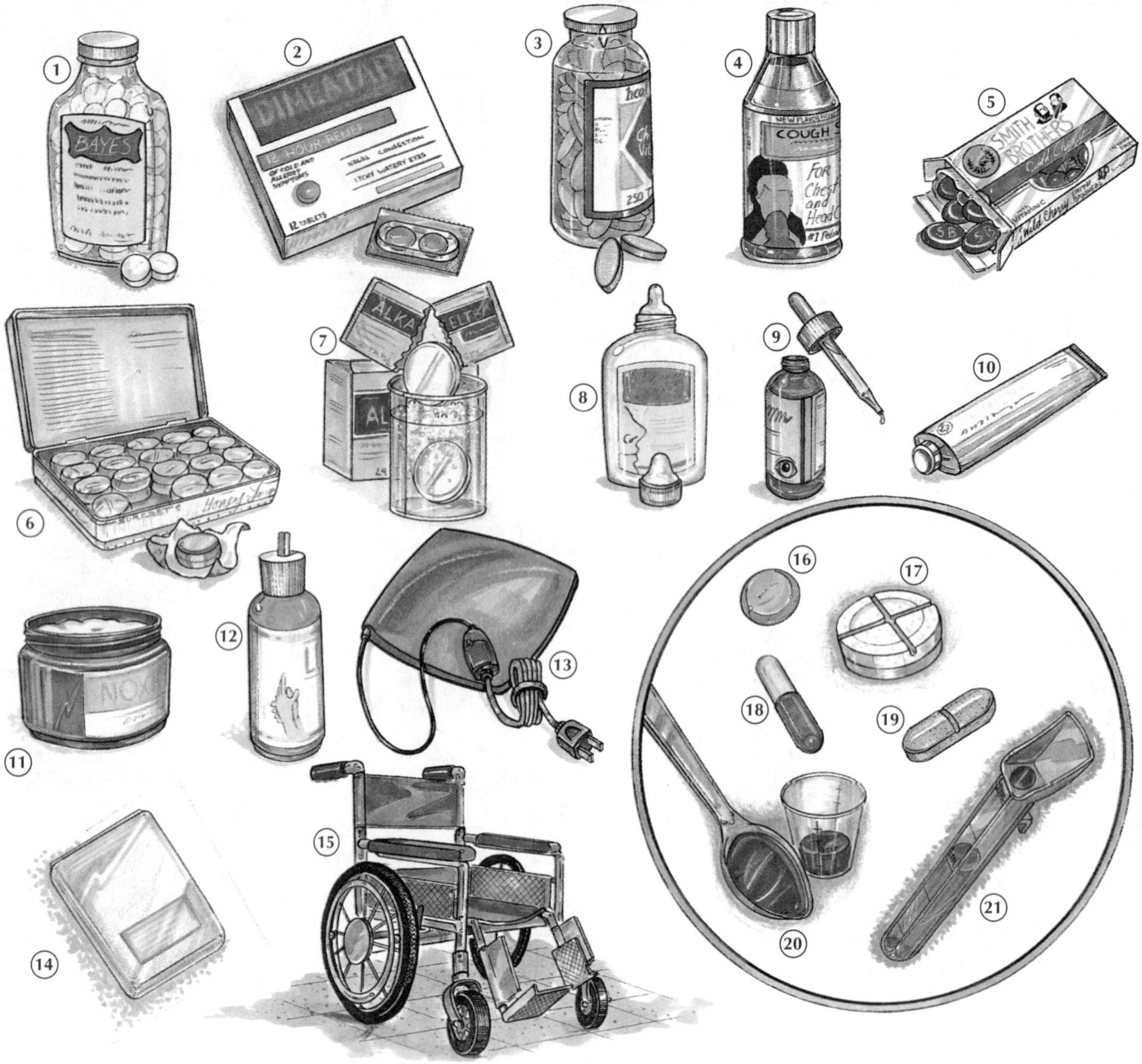

1. aspirin 아스피린
2. cold tablets 정제감기약
3. vitamins 비타민제
4. cough syrup 기침시럽 / 시럽제 기침약
5. cough drops 기침을 멎게하는 드롭스/ 기침캔디
6. throat lozenges 목캔디
7. antacid tablets 제산정 / 제산제
8. decongestant spray/nasal spray 비염용 스프레이 / 코막힘 해소 스프레이 / 충혈 완화제
9. eye drops 안약
10. ointment 연고
11. creme 크림
12. lotion 로션
13. heating pad 찜질 패드
14. ice pack 냉찜질 팩
15. wheelchair 휠체어
16. pill 알약
17. tablet 정제
18. capsule 캡슐
19. caplet 캐플릿
20. teaspoon 티 스푼
21. tablespoon 테이블 스푼

[1–15] A. What did the doctor say?
B. { She/He told me to take [1–4].
She/He told me to use (a/an) [5–15].

[16–21] A. What's the dosage?
B. One ______, every three hours.

What medicines do you take or use?
For what ailments?

Describe any medical treatments or medicines in your country that are different from the ones in these lessons.

우체국

편지 **1.** letter
엽서 **2.** postcard
항공우편용 봉함편지 **3.** air letter/ aerogramme
소포 **4.** package/parcel
1종우편 **5.** first class
항공우편 **6.** air mail
소포우편 **7.** parcel post
서적우편 3종우편 **8.** book rate/third class
등기우편 **9.** registered mail
속달우편 **10.** express mail/ overnight mail

우표 **11.** stamp
50장짜리 우표 시트 **12.** sheet of stamps
우표 말이 / 우표 롤 **13.** roll of stamps
20장짜리 우표묶음 **14.** book of stamps
우편환 **15.** money order
주소변경통지서 **16.** change-of-address form
특별서비스 신청서 **17.** selective service registration form
봉투 **18.** envelope
주소 **19.** address
우편번호 **20.** zip code
반환주소 **21.** return address

우표 **22.** stamp/postage
소인 **23.** postmark
우편물 넣는곳 **24.** mail slot
창구 **25.** window
우체국 직원 **26.** postal worker/ postal clerk
저울 **27.** scale
우표 자동판매기 **28.** stamp machine
우편물 배달차량 **29.** mail truck
우체통 **30.** mailbox
우편 집배원 **31.** letter carrier/ mail carrier
우편낭 **32.** mail bag

[1–4]
A. Where are you going?
B. To the post office.
I have to mail a/an _______.

[5–10]
A. How do you want to send it?
B. _______, please.

[11–17]
A. Next!
B. I'd like a _______, please.
A. Here you are.

[19–22]
A. Do you want me to mail this letter for you?
B. Yes, thanks.
A. Oops! You forgot the _______!

What time does your letter carrier deliver your mail? Does he/she drive a mail truck or carry a mail bag and walk?

Describe the post office you use:
How many postal windows are there?
Is there a stamp machine?
Are the postal workers friendly?

Tell about the postal system in your country.

THE LIBRARY
도서관

사서	**1.** librarian	참고실 사서	**11.** reference librarian	신문	**22.** newspaper
대출하는 곳	**2.** checkout desk	참고 자료실	**12.** reference section	잡지	**23.** magazine
보조사서	**3.** library assistant	지도(책)	**13.** atlas	저널	**24.** journal
마이크로 필름	**4.** microfilm	백과사전	**14.** encyclopedia	도서분류카드	**25.** call card
마이크로 피시	**5.** microfiche	사전	**15.** dictionary	도서분류번호	**26.** call number
도서목록 카드	**6.** card catalog	시청각자료실	**16.** media section	저자	**27.** author
온라인 도서목록	**7.** online catalog	비디오	**17.** videotape	제목	**28.** title
선반	**8.** shelves	레코드	**18.** record	주제	**29.** subject
안내 데스크	**9.** information desk	테이프	**19.** tape	도서대출증	**30.** library card
복사기	**10.** copier/(photo)copy machine	컴퓨터 디스켓	**20.** computer diskette		
		정기간행물실	**21.** periodicals section		

[1–11]
A. Excuse me. Where's/ Where are the _______?
B. Over there, at/near/next to the _______.

[12–24]
A. Excuse me. Where can I find a/an [13–15, 17–20, 22–24]?
B. Look in the [12, 16, 21] over there.

[27–29]
A. May I help you?
B. Yes, please. I'm having trouble finding a book.
A. Do you know the _______?
B. Yes. …………

Do you go to a library? Which one? What does this library have? Describe how you use the library.

THE SCHOOL
학교

- 교무실 **1.** office
- 양호실 **2.** nurse's office
- 진로 상담실 **3.** guidance office
- 학교식당 **4.** cafeteria
- 교장실 **5.** principal's office
- 교실 **6.** classroom
- 사물함 **7.** locker
- 언어실습실 / 시청각실 **8.** language lab
- 실험실 **9.** chemistry lab
- 교직원 휴게실 **10.** teachers' lounge
- 체육관 **11.** gym/gymnasium
- 탈의실 **12.** locker room
- 강당 **13.** auditorium
- 운동장 **14.** field
- 관람석 **15.** bleachers
- 트랙 **16.** track
- 교장 **17.** principal
- 교감 **18.** assistant principal
- 양호교사 **19.** (school) nurse
- 진로상담 교사 **20.** guidance counselor
- 식당관리 교사 **21.** lunchroom monitor
- 학교식당 종업원 **22.** cafeteria worker
- 운전교습 교사 **23.** driver's ed instructor
- 교사 **24.** teacher
- 코치 **25.** coach
- 시설관리인 **26.** custodian

[1–16] A. Where are you going?
B. I'm going to the ________.*
A. Do you have a hall pass?
B. Yes. Here it is.

With 6 and 7, use: I'm going to my ______.

[17–26] A. Who's that?
B. That's the new ________.

Describe the school where you study English.
Tell about the rooms, offices, and people.

Tell about differences between schools in the United States and in your country.

학과목 및 과외활동

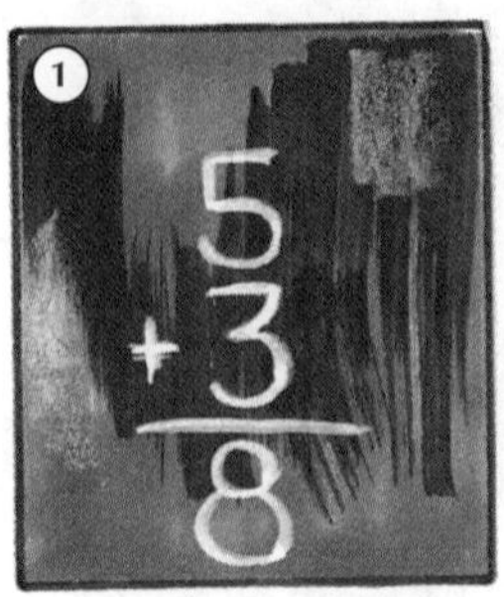

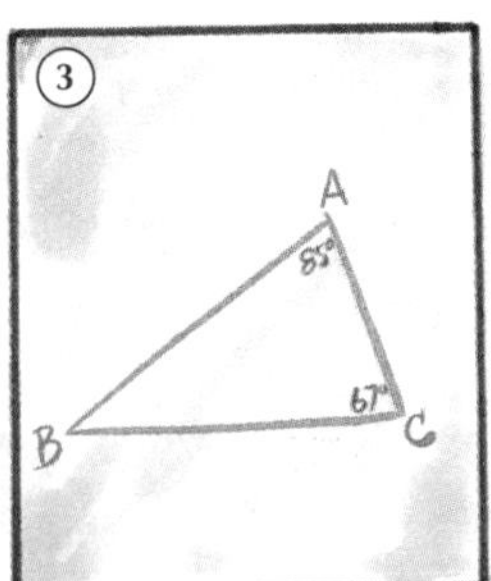

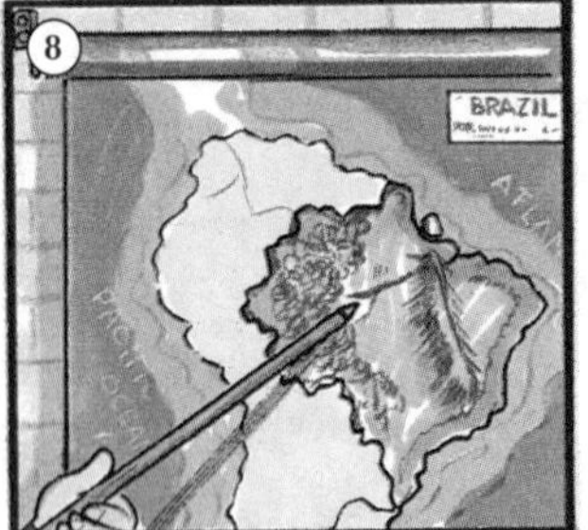

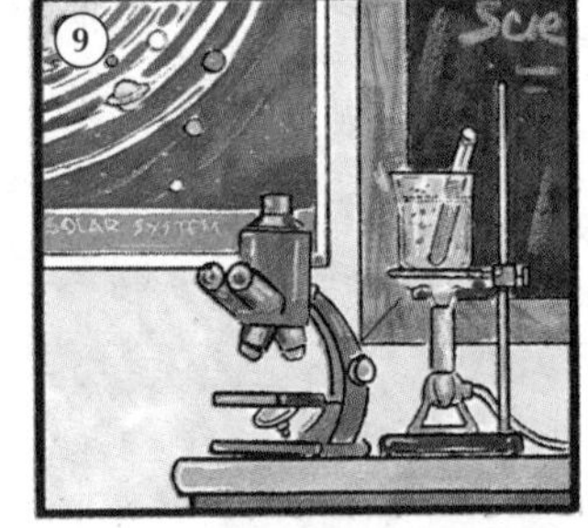

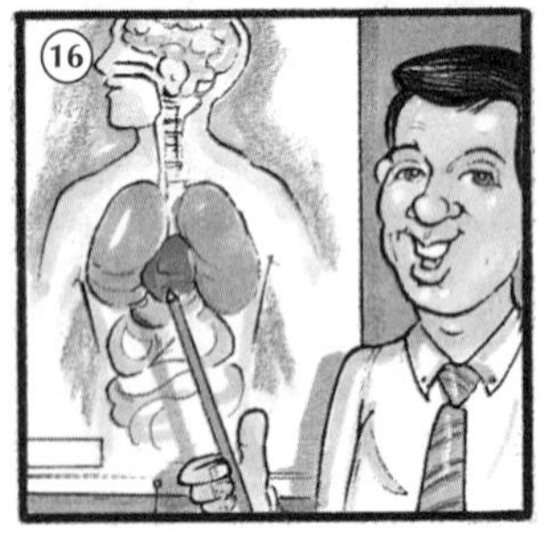

수학 **1.** math/mathematics
대수 **2.** algebra
기하학 **3.** geometry
삼각법 **4.** trigonometry
미적분 **5.** calculus
영어 **6.** English
역사 **7.** history
지리 **8.** geography

과학 **9.** science
생물 **10.** biology
화학 **11.** chemistry
물리 **12.** physics
스페인어 **13.** Spanish
불어 **14.** French
가정학 **15.** home economics
보건위생 **16.** health

공예 **17.** industrial arts/shop
운전소양교육 **18.** driver's education/driver's ed
타자 **19.** typing
미술 **20.** art
음악 **21.** music

밴드부 **22.** band
관현악단 **23.** orchestra
합창반 **24.** choir/chorus
연극반 **25.** drama
미식축구부 **26.** football

교보 / 학교신문 **27.** school newspaper
졸업앨범 **28.** yearbook
문예지 **29.** literary magazine
학생회 **30.** student government

[1–21]
A. What do you have next period?
B. ________. How about you?
A. ________.
B. There's the bell. I've got to go.

[22–30]
A. Are you going home right after school?
B. { No. I have [22–26] practice.
{ No. I have a [27–30] meeting.

What is/was your favorite subject? Why? What extracurricular activities do/did you participate in?

OCCUPATIONS I
직업 I

A. What do you do?
B. I'm an **accountant**. How about you?
A. I'm a **carpenter**.

회계사	**1.** accountant	조립공	**6.** assembler	버스 운전기사	**11.** bus driver
남자배우	**2.** actor	제과(제빵) 기술자	**7.** baker	푸줏간 주인	**12.** butcher
여자배우	**3.** actress	이용사	**8.** barber	목수	**13.** carpenter
건축기사	**4.** architect	회계원	**9.** bookkeeper	계산원	**14.** cashier
화가	**5.** artist	벽돌공	**10.** bricklayer/mason	주방장 / 요리사	**15.** chef/cook

컴퓨터 프로그래머 **16.** computer programmer
공사장 인부 **17.** construction worker
우편배달부 **18.** courier/messenger
관리인 / 수위 **19.** custodian/janitor
정보처리기사 **20.** data processor

배달원 **21.** delivery person
전기기사 **22.** electrician
농부 **23.** farmer
소방수 **24.** firefighter
어부 **25.** fisherman

십장 / 공사장 현장감독 **26.** foreman
정원사 **27.** gardener
미용사 **28.** hairdresser
가정부 **29.** housekeeper
기자 **30.** journalist/reporter

[At a job interview]
A. Are you an experienced ________?
B. Yes. I'm a very experienced ________.

A. How long have you been a/an ________?
B. I've been a/an ________ for .... months/years.

Which of these occupations do you think are the most interesting? the most difficult? Why?

직업 II

A. What's your occupation?
B. I'm a **lawyer**.
A. A **lawyer**?
B. Yes. That's right.

변호사 **1.** lawyer
기계공 **2.** mechanic
모델 **3.** model
뉴스 캐스터 **4.** newscaster
페인트공 **5.** painter

약사 **6.** pharmacist
사진사 **7.** photographer
비행기 조종사 **8.** pilot
배관공 **9.** plumber
경찰 **10.** police officer

부동산 중개인 **11.** real estate agent
안내원 **12.** receptionist
수리공 **13.** repairperson
점원 / 판매원 **14.** salesperson
환경 미화원 **15.** sanitation worker

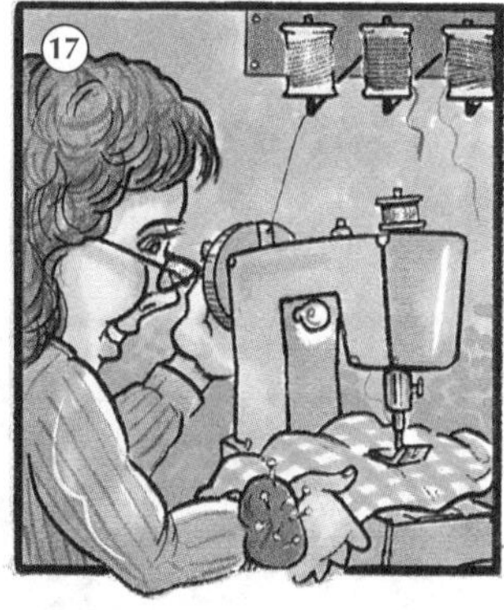

과학자 **16.** scientist
재봉사 **17.** seamstress
비서 **18.** secretary
경비원 **19.** security guard
창고 담당(인) **20.** stock clerk

재단사 **21.** tailor
택시 운전기사 **22.** taxi driver
교사 **23.** teacher
통역사 **24.** translator/interpreter
여행사직원 **25.** travel agent

트럭 운전기사 **26.** truck driver
웨이터 / 급사 **27.** waiter
웨이트리스 / 여급 **28.** waitress
용접공 **29.** welder
수의사 **30.** veterinarian

A. Are you still a ________?
B. No. I'm a ________.
A. Oh. That's interesting.

A. What kind of job would you like in the future?
B. I'd like to be a ________.

Do you work? What's your occupation?
What are the occupations of people in your family?

작업 활동

A. Can you **act**?
B. Yes, I can.

연기하다 **1.** act
(부품을) 조립하다 **2.** assemble *components*
(빵을) 굽다 **3.** bake
(물건을) 만들다 / 짓다 **4.** build *things*/ construct *things*

청소하다 **5.** clean
요리하다 **6.** cook
(피자를) 배달하다 **7.** deliver *pizzas*
(건 물을) 설계하다 **8.** design *buildings*
그리다 **9.** draw

(트럭을) 운전하다 **10.** drive *a truck*
서류철하다 **11.** file
(비행기를) 조종하다 **12.** fly *an airplane*
(야채를) 기르다 **13.** grow *vegetables*
(건물을) 경비하다 **14.** guard *buildings*

(잔디를) 깎다 **15.** mow *lawns*
(장비를) 운전하다 **16.** operate *equipment*
페인트 칠하다 **17.** paint
(피아노를) 연주하다 **18.** play the *piano*
(물건을) 수리하다 **19.** repair *things*/fix *things*
(자동차를) 팔다 **20.** sell *cars*
(음식을) 나르다 **21.** serve *food*

바느질하다 **22.** sew
노래하다 **23.** sing
가르치다 **24.** teach
통역하다 **25.** translate
타이프치다 **26.** type
(접시를) 닦다 **27.** wash *dishes*
저술하다 **28.** write

A. What do you do for a living?
B. I _______.

A. Do you know how to _______?
B. Yes. I've been _______ing for years.

Tell about your work abilities.
What can you do?

사무실

안내 데스크	1.	reception area
옷걸이 / 코트걸이	2.	coat rack
옷장	3.	coat closet
게시판	4.	message board
우편함	5.	mailbox
서류 캐비닛	6.	file cabinet
사무용품 캐비닛	7.	supply cabinet
비품 캐비닛	8.	storage cabinet
작업대	9.	workstation
컴퓨터 작업대	10.	computer workstation
냉수기	11.	water cooler
커피 카트	12.	coffee cart
사무실	13.	office
우편 수발실	14.	mailroom
우편요금 별납 인쇄기	15.	postage machine/postage meter
복사기	16.	copier/(photo)copy machine
휴지통	17.	waste receptacle
사무용품실	18.	supply room
창고 / 비품실	19.	storage room
회의실	20.	conference room
회의용테이블	21.	conference table
화이트 보드	22.	whiteboard/dry erase board
직원 휴게실	23.	employee lounge
커피 자판기	24.	coffee machine
음료수 자동판매기	25.	soda machine
안내원	26.	receptionist
타자수	27.	typist
자료정리원	28.	file clerk
비서	29.	secretary
사무보조원	30.	administrative assistant
사무실 지배인	31.	office manager
사무실 보조원	32.	office assistant
고용주 / 사장	33.	employer/boss

[1–25] A. Where's ....?

B { He's/She's in the/his/her ________.*
  He's/She's at the/his/her ________.†

*1, 13, 14, 18–20, 23 †2–12, 15–17, 21, 22, 24, 25

[26–33] A. Who's he/she?

B. He's/She's the new ________.

사무기기

A. Do you know how to work this **computer**?
B. No, I don't.
A. Let me show you how.

컴퓨터	**1.** computer
단말기	**2.** VDT/video display terminal
(도트 매트릭스) 프린터	**3.** (dot-matrix) printer
(레터 퀄리티) 프린터	**4.** (letter-quality) printer
(레이저) 프린터	**5.** (laser) printer
워드프로세서	**6.** word processor
타자기	**7.** typewriter
(전자) 계산기	**8.** calculator
업소용 계산기	**9.** adding machine
소형녹음기	**10.** microcassette recorder/dictaphone
전화	**11.** telephone
헤드폰	**12.** headset
자동 (전화) 교환기	**13.** phone system
텔렉스	**14.** telex machine
팩스	**15.** fax machine
연필깎는 기계	**16.** pencil sharpener
자동 연필깎기	**17.** electric pencil sharpener
종이 절단기	**18.** paper cutter
플라스틱 바인딩기	**19.** plastic binding machine
우편 저울	**20.** postal scale
파쇄기 / 문서 세단기	**21.** paper shredder

A. I think this ________ is broken!
B. I'll take a look at it.

A. Have you seen the new ________?
B. No, I haven't.
A. It's much better than the old one!

Do you know how to operate a computer? a fax machine? Give step-by-step instructions for using some type of office equipment.

OFFICE FURNISHINGS
사무가구

책상	1.	desk
회전의자	2.	swivel chair
명함철 / 롤로덱스	3.	rolodex
연필꽂이	4.	pencil cup
결재서류함	5.	letter tray/ stacking tray
메모지함	6.	memo holder
책상 달력	7.	desk calendar
책상 램프	8.	desk lamp
명패	9.	nameplate
책상 패드	10.	desk pad
휴지통	11.	wastebasket
사무용 의자	12.	posture chair/ clerical chair
벽걸이 달력	13.	wall calendar
월간계획표	14.	wall planner
서류캐비넷	15.	file cabinet
호치치스	16.	stapler
스테이플 제거기 / 꺾쇠 제거기	17.	staple remover
테이프 절단기	18.	tape dispenser
자석클립 통	19.	paper clip dispenser
명함	20.	business cards
필기 받침대	21.	clipboard
업무수첩	22.	appointment book
수첩	23.	organizer/ personal planner
월간계획표	24.	timesheet
급여 / 봉급	25.	paycheck
편지오프너	26.	letter opener
가위	27.	scissors
천공기	28.	punch
3구 천공기	29.	3-hole punch
스탬프 패드 / 잉크 패드	30.	stamp pad/ink pad
고무 스탬프	31.	rubber stamp
펜	32.	pen
연필	33.	pencil
샤프펜슬	34.	mechanical pencil
형광펜	35.	highlighter (pen)
지우개	36.	eraser

[1–15]
A. Welcome to the company.
B. Thank you.
A. How do you like your ______?
B. It's/They're very nice.

[16–36]
A. My desk is such a mess! I can't find my ______!
B. Here it is/Here they are next to your ______.

Which items on this page do you have? Do you have an appointment book, personal planner, or calendar? How do you remember important things such as appointments, meetings, and birthdays?

사무용품

클립	**1.** paper clip	포스트 잇	**13.** Post-It note pad	고무풀	**25.** rubber cement
플라스틱 클립	**2.** plastic clip	전화 메모지	**14.** message pad	매스킹테이프 / 보호테이프	**26.** masking tape
물림쇠	**3.** paper fastener	리걸 사이즈 용지	**15.** legal pad	스카치 테이프	**27.** Scotch tape/ cellophane tape
불독 클립	**4.** bulldog clip	화일 홀더 / 서류철	**16.** file folder/ manila folder	포장테이프 / 소포용 테이프	**28.** sealing tape/ package mailing tape
바인더 클립	**5.** binder clip	편지봉투	**17.** envelope	편지지	**29.** stationery
클램프	**6.** clamp	카달로그 봉투	**18.** catalog envelope	타자용지	**30.** typing paper
고무줄	**7.** rubber band	물림쇠가 있는 봉투	**19.** clasp envelope	카본지	**31.** carbon paper
호치키스 알 / 꺽쇠	**8.** staple	우편봉투	**20.** mailer	컴퓨터용지	**32.** computer paper
압정	**9.** thumbtack	우편라벨	**21.** mailing label	수정액	**33.** correction fluid
압핀	**10.** pushpin	타자기 리본	**22.** typewriter ribbon		
색인카드	**11.** index card	고체풀	**23.** gluestick		
공책	**12.** memo pad/ note pad	풀 / 접착제	**24.** glue		

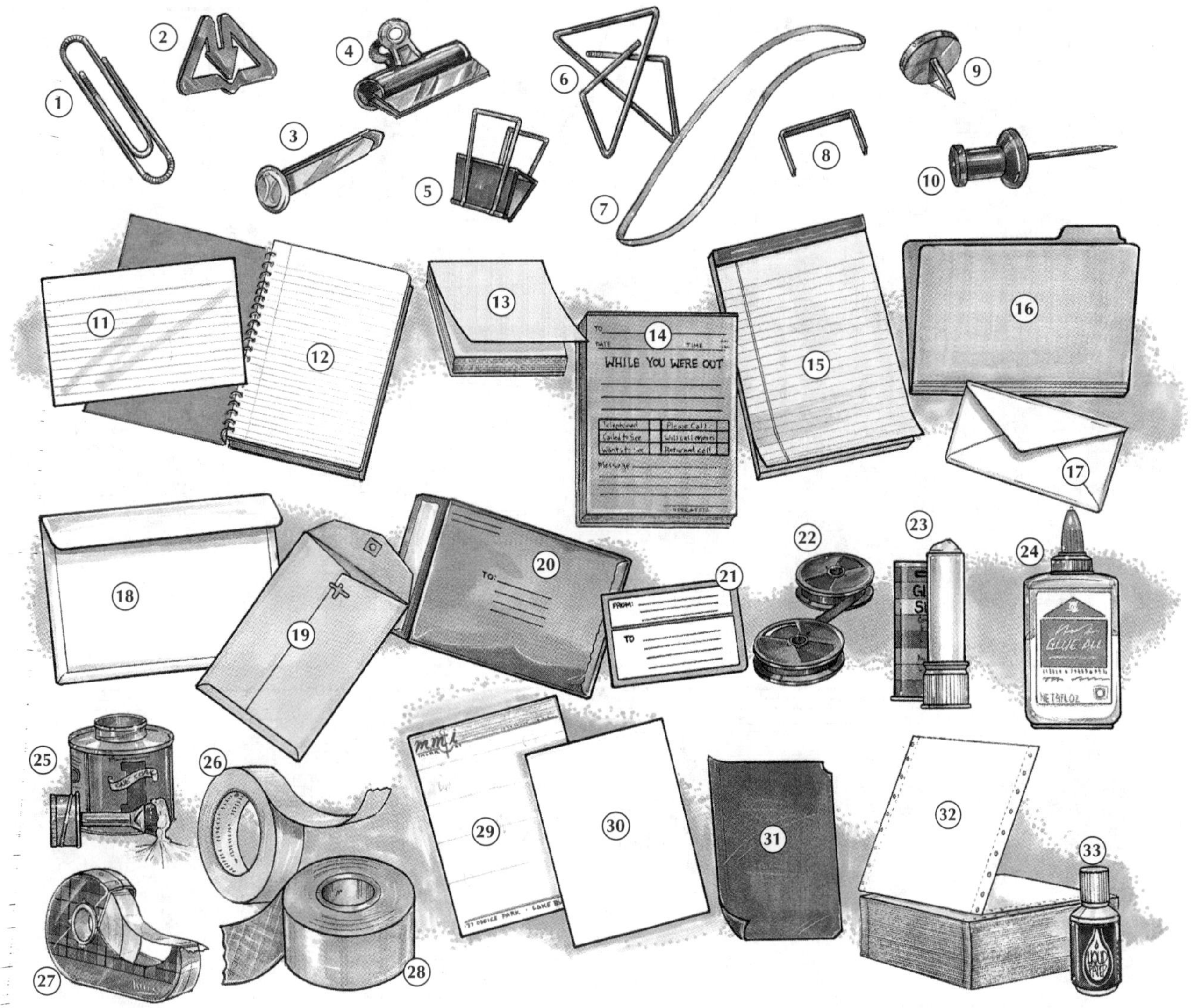

A. We've run out of [1–23]s.
We've run out of [24–33].

B. I'll get some more from the supply room.

A. Could I borrow a/an/some [1–33]?

B. Sure. Here you are.

THE FACTORY
공장

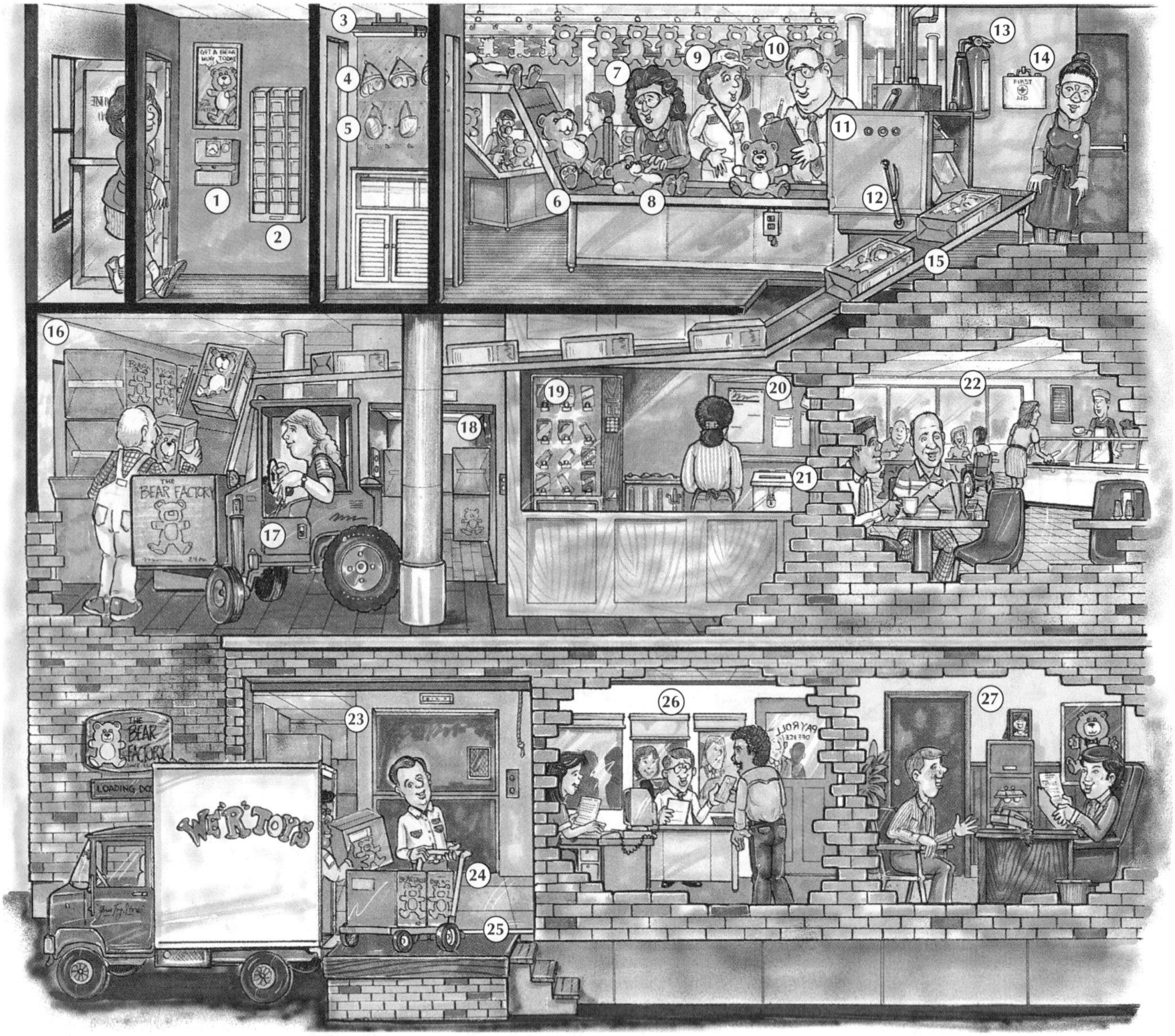

1. time clock 출퇴근시간 기록기
2. time cards 근무시간 기록표
3. supply room 비품실
4. safety glasses 보안경
5. masks 마스크
6. (assembly) line (조립) 라인
7. worker 직공
8. work station 작업대
9. quality control supervisor 품질관리감독원
10. foreman 십장 / 공사장 현장감독
11. machine 기계
12. lever 레버
13. fire extinguisher 소화기
14. first-aid kit 응급처치 약품함
15. conveyor belt 물품 자동 이동기 / 컨베이어
16. warehouse 창고
17. forklift 지게차
18. freight elevator 화물용 엘리베이터
19. vending machine 자판기 / 자동 판매기
20. union notice 노조 게시판
21. suggestion box 건의함
22. cafeteria 구내식당
23. shipping department 출고부서
24. hand truck 화물운반용 손수레
25. loading dock 적재장
26. payroll office 경리부
27. personnel office 인사부

A. Excuse me. I'm a new employee. Where's/Where are the ________?
B. Next to/Near/In/On the ________.

A. Have you seen *Fred*?
B. Yes. He's in/on/at/next to/near the ________.

Are there any factories where you live? What kind? What are the working conditions there?

What products do factories in your country produce?

THE CONSTRUCTION SITE
공사장

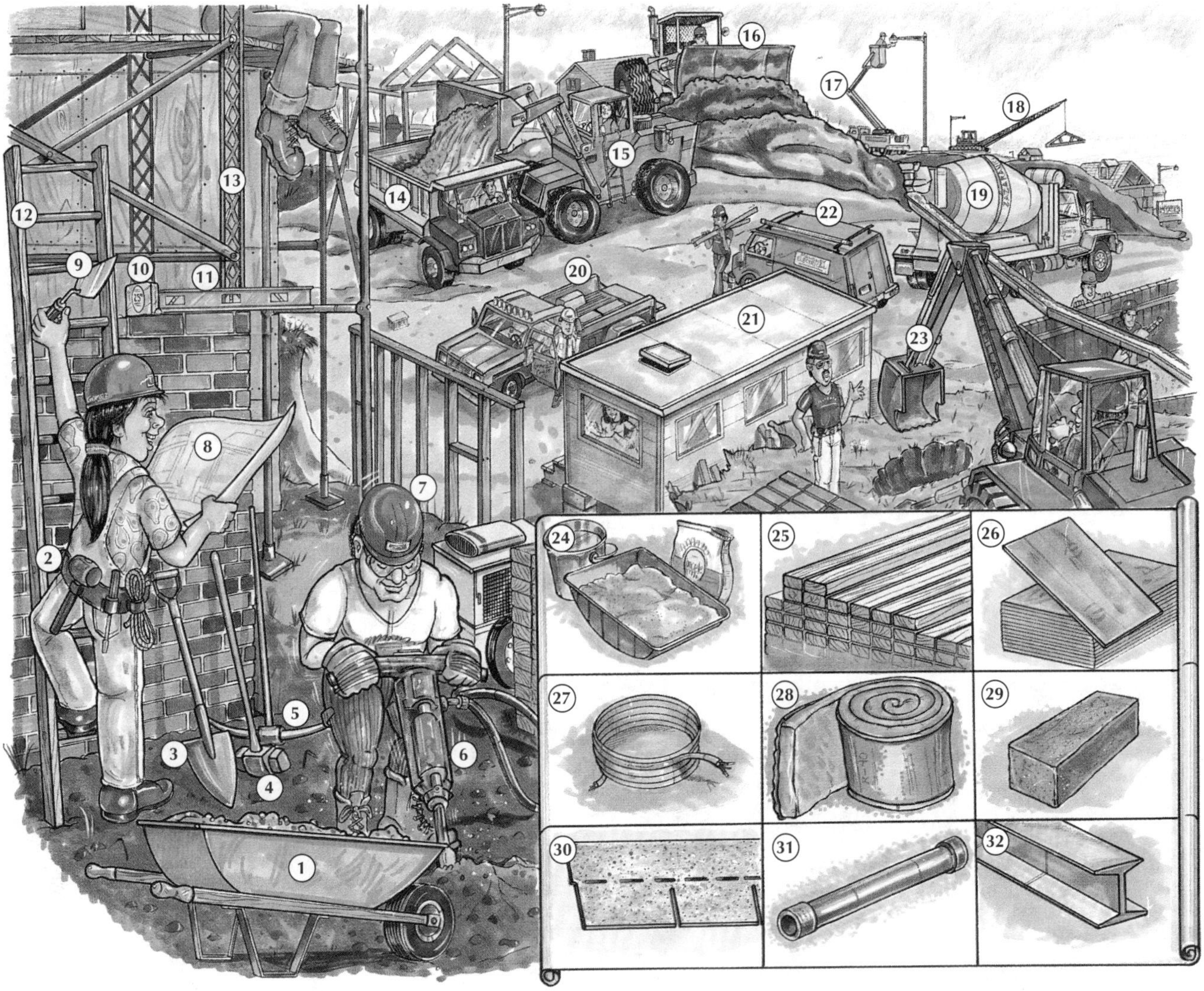

외바퀴 손수레	**1.** wheelbarrow
공구벨트	**2.** toolbelt
삽	**3.** shovel
큰 망치	**4.** sledgehammer
곡괭이	**5.** pickax
착암용 드릴	**6.** jackhammer/ pneumatic drill
헬멧 / 안전모	**7.** helmet/hard hat
설계도	**8.** blueprints
흙손	**9.** trowel
줄자	**10.** tape measure
수평기	**11.** level
사다리	**12.** ladder
비계목	**13.** scaffolding
덤프 트럭	**14.** dump truck
적재기	**15.** front-end loader
불도저	**16.** bulldozer
체리픽커	**17.** cherry picker
크레인 / 기중기	**18.** crane
레미콘 트럭	**19.** cement mixer
픽업 트럭	**20.** pickup truck
트레일러	**21.** trailer
밴	**22.** van
포클레인 / 굴착기	**23.** backhoe
시멘트	**24.** cement
목재 / 제재목	**25.** wood/lumber
합판 / 베니아판	**26.** plywood
전선	**27.** wire
단열재 / 절연체	**28.** insulation
벽돌	**29.** brick
지붕 널	**30.** shingle
파이프	**31.** pipe
도리 / 빔	**32.** girder/beam

[1–12]
A. Could you get me that/those ______?
B. Sure.

[13–23]
A. Watch out for that ______!
B. Oh! Thanks for the warning!

[24–32]
A. Are we going to have enough [24–28] / [29–32] s to finish the job?
B. I think so.

자동차

전조등	**1.**	headlight
범퍼	**2.**	bumper
방향지시등	**3.**	turn signal
주차등	**4.**	parking light
타이어	**5.**	tire
휠캡	**6.**	hubcap
후드	**7.**	hood
앞 유리창	**8.**	windshield
와이퍼	**9.**	windshield wipers
측면거울	**10.**	side mirror
안테나	**11.**	antenna
선루프	**12.**	sunroof
화물고정대	**13.**	luggage rack/ luggage carrier
뒷 유리창	**14.**	rear windshield
뒷 열선	**15.**	rear defroster

트렁크	**16.**	trunk
후미등	**17.**	taillight
브레이크등	**18.**	brake light
후진등	**19.**	backup light
번호판	**20.**	license plate
배기관	**21.**	tailpipe
머플러	**22.**	muffler
트랜스미션	**23.**	transmission
연료탱크	**24.**	gas tank
잭	**25.**	jack
스페어 타이어 / 예비 타이어	**26.**	spare tire
플레어	**27.**	flare
점퍼 케이블	**28.**	jumper cables
엔진	**29.**	engine
점화플러그	**30.**	spark plugs
카뷰레터	**31.**	carburetor

에어 필터	**32.**	air filter
배터리	**33.**	battery
오일 계측봉	**34.**	dipstick
발전기	**35.**	alternator
라디에이터	**36.**	radiator
팬 벨트	**37.**	fan belt
라디에이터 호스	**38.**	radiator hose
주유소	**39.**	gas station/ service station
공기펌프	**40.**	air pump
정비구역	**41.**	service bay
자동차 수리공	**42.**	mechanic
주유소 종업원	**43.**	attendant
주유펌프	**44.**	gas pump
노즐	**45.**	nozzle

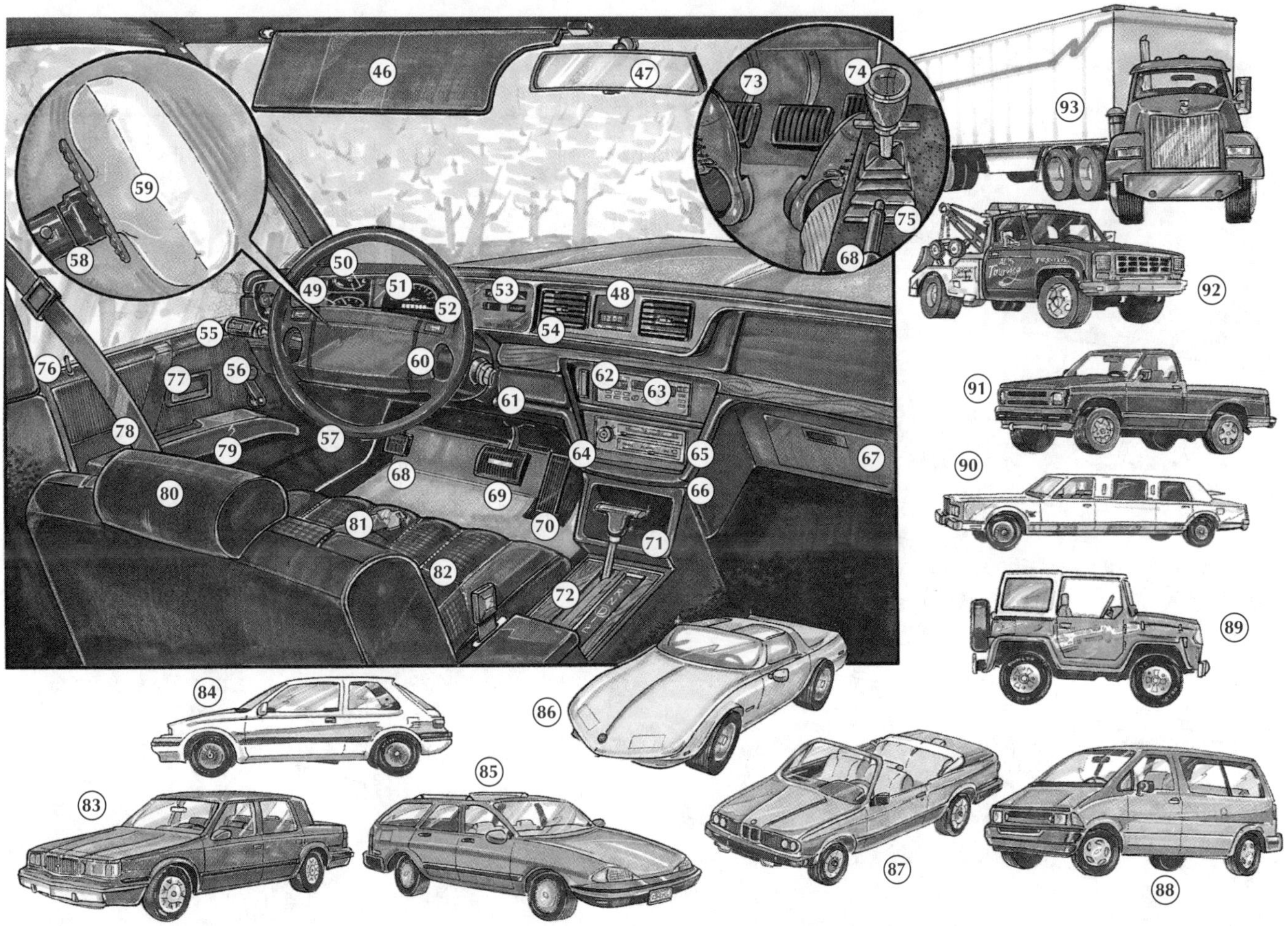

햇빛 가리개 **46.** visor
백미러 **47.** rearview mirror
계기판 **48.** dashboard/ instrument panel
연료계기판 **49.** gas gauge/ fuel gauge
온도계 **50.** temperature gauge
속도계기판 **51.** speedometer
주행거리계기판 **52.** odometer
비상등 **53.** warning lights
통풍구 **54.** vent
방향 지시기 **55.** turn signal
주행속도 자동조절장치 **56.** cruise control
운전대 **57.** steering wheel
운전대 축 **58.** steering column
에어백 **59.** air bag
경적 / 클랙슨 **60.** horn
점화장치 **61.** ignition

라디오 **62.** radio
카세트 / 테이프덱 **63.** tape deck/ cassette player
에어컨 **64.** air conditioning
히터 **65.** heater
뒷 열선 **66.** defroster
사물함 **67.** glove compartment
비상 브레이크 **68.** emergency brake
브레이크 **69.** brake
액셀러레이터 **70.** accelerator/ gas pedal
변속레버 **71.** gearshift
자동변속장치 **72.** automatic transmission
클러치 **73.** clutch
수동변속레버 **74.** stickshift
수동변속장치 **75.** manual transmission

도어 록 **76.** door lock
차문 손잡이 **77.** door handle
안전벨트 / 어깨벨트 **78.** shoulder harness
팔걸이 **79.** armrest
머리받침대 **80.** headrest
좌석벨트 **81.** seat belt
좌석 **82.** seat
세단 **83.** sedan
해치백 **84.** hatchback
스테이션 웨곤 **85.** station wagon
스포츠 카 **86.** sports car
컨버터블 **87.** convertible
미니밴 **88.** minivan
지프 **89.** jeep
리무진 **90.** limousine
픽업 트럭 **91.** pick-up truck
견인차 **92.** tow truck
트럭 **93.** truck

[1, 3, 8–15, 23, 34–38, 46–82]
A. What's the matter with your car?
B. The ________(s) is/are broken.

[1, 4–6, 9–11, 30–33, 37, 38]
A. Can I help you?
B. Yes. I need to replace a/the ________(s).

[1, 2, 4–8, 10–14, 16–20]
A. I was just in a car accident!
B. Oh, no! Were you hurt?
A. No. But my ________(s) was/were damaged.

HIGHWAYS AND STREETS
고속도로와 거리

터널	**1.** tunnel	1차선	**14.** left lane	일방통행로	**27.** one-way street
다리	**2.** bridge	2차선	**15.** middle lane/ center lane	중앙선	**28.** double yellow line
통행료 징수소	**3.** tollbooth	3차선	**16.** right lane	횡단보도	**29.** crosswalk
정액요금차선	**4.** exact change lane	갓길 / 노견	**17.** shoulder	교차로	**30.** intersection
도로표지판	**5.** route sign	점선	**18.** broken line	학교앞 건널목	**31.** school crossing
고속도로	**6.** highway	실선	**19.** solid line	코너	**32.** corner
도로	**7.** road	속도제한 표지	**20.** speed limit sign	신호등	**33.** traffic light/ traffic signal
중앙분리대	**8.** divider/barrier	출구	**21.** exit (ramp)	좌회전 금지표지	**34.** no left turn sign
고가도로	**9.** overpass	출구표지	**22.** exit sign	우회전 금지표지	**35.** no right turn sign
지하도로	**10.** underpass	양보표지	**23.** yield sign	유 — 턴 금지표지	**36.** no U-turn sign
진입로	**11.** entrance ramp/ on ramp	휴게소	**24.** service area	진입금지표지	**37.** do not enter sign
주간고속도로	**12.** interstate (highway)	철도건널목	**25.** railroad crossing	우선멈춤표지	**38.** stop sign
중앙분리대	**13.** median	거리	**26.** street		

A. Where's the accident?

B. It's on/in/at/near the ______.

Describe a highway you travel on.
Describe an intersection near where you live.

In your area, on which highways and streets do most accidents occur? Why are these places dangerous?

대중교통

기차 **A. train**
- 기차역 **1.** train station
- 매표소 **2.** ticket window
- 착발 안내판 **3.** arrival and departure board
- 안내 데스크 **4.** information booth
- 열차운행 시간표 **5.** schedule/timetable
- 기차 **6.** train
- 선로 **7.** track
- 플랫폼 **8.** platform
- 승객 **9.** passenger
- 안내원 / 차장 **10.** conductor
- 수하물 **11.** luggage/baggage
- 수하물 운반인 **12.** porter/redcap
- 엔진 **13.** engine
- 기관사 **14.** engineer
- 객실 **15.** passenger car
- 침대차 **16.** sleeper
- 식당차 **17.** dining car

버스 **B. bus**
- 버스 **18.** bus
- 수하물칸 **19.** luggage compartment/ baggage compartment
- 버스 운전기사 **20.** bus driver
- 버스 터미널 **21.** bus station
- 매표소 **22.** ticket counter

시내버스 **C. local bus**
- 버스 정류장 **23.** bus stop
- 승객 **24.** rider/passenger
- 요금 **25.** (bus) fare
- 요금통 **26.** fare box
- 환승권 **27.** transfer

지하철 **D. subway**
- 지하철 역 **28.** subway station
- 지하철 **29.** subway
- 매표소 **30.** token booth
- 회전식 출입문 **31.** turnstile
- 통근승객 **32.** commuter
- (지하철) 토큰 **33.** (subway) token
- 승차표 **34.** fare card
- 발권기 / 발매기 **35.** fare card machine

택시 **E. taxi**
- 택시 승강장 **36.** taxi stand
- 택시 **37.** taxi/cab/taxicab
- 미터기 **38.** meter
- 요금 **39.** fare
- 택시 운전기사 **40.** cab driver/taxi driver

[A–E]
A. How are you going to get there?
B. { I'm going to take the [A–D] .
I'm going to take a [E] .

[1–8, 10–23, 26, 28–31, 35, 36]
A. Excuse me. Where's the ________?
B. Over there.

THE AIRPORT
공항

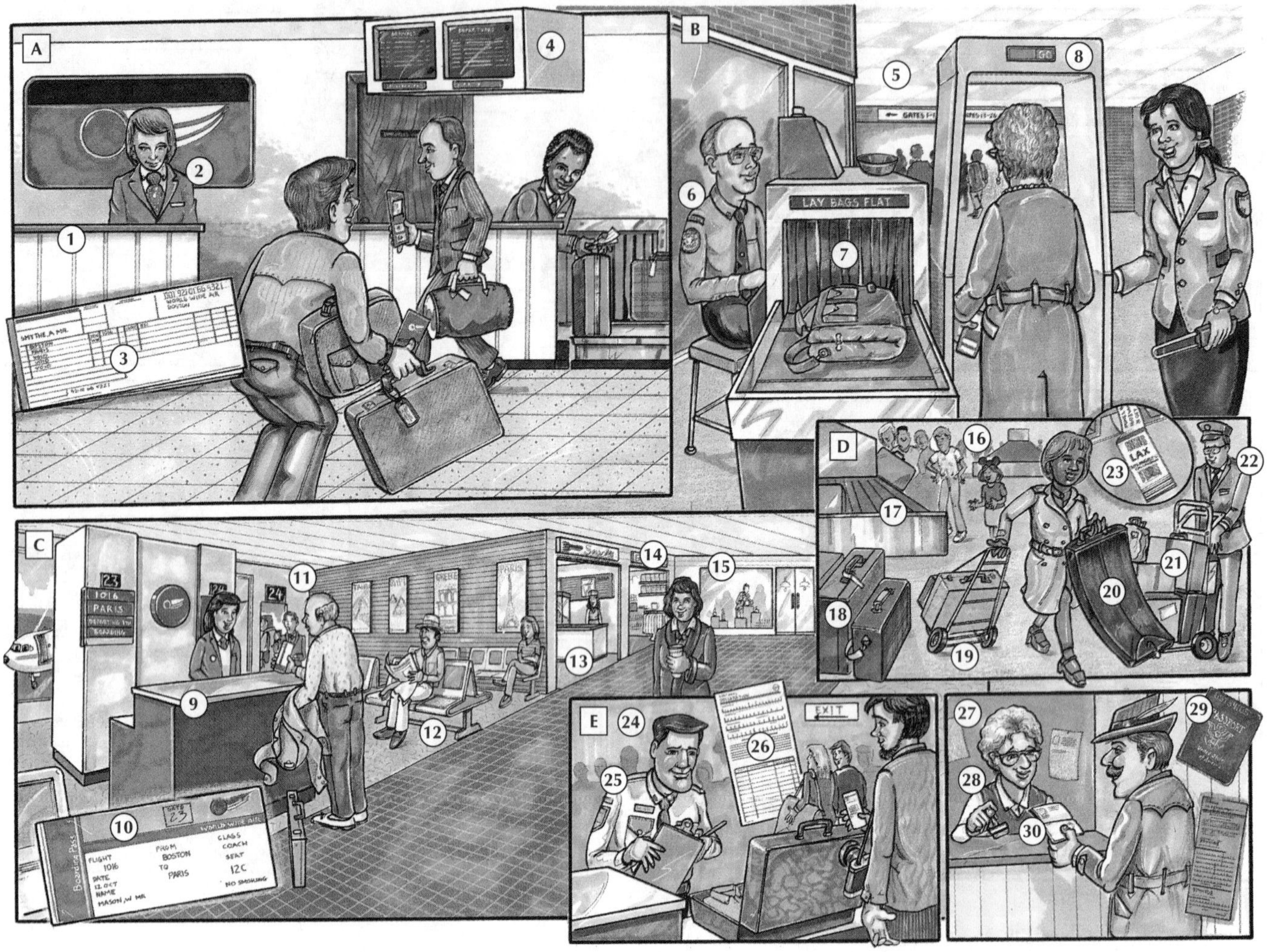

체크 인 — A. Check-In

- 발권창구 — 1. ticket counter
- 발매인 — 2. ticket agent
- 비행기표 — 3. ticket
- 착발 모니터 — 4. arrival and departure monitor

보안 검색 — B. Security

- 보안 검색대 — 5. security checkpoint
- 보안 검색원 — 6. security guard
- 엑스레이기 — 7. X-ray machine
- 금속탐지기 — 8. metal detector

탑승구 — C. The Gate

- 체크 인 카운터 — 9. check-in counter
- 탑승권 — 10. boarding pass
- 탑승구 — 11. gate
- 대기실 — 12. waiting area
- 매점 / 스넥코너 — 13. concession stand/snack bar
- 선물가게 — 14. gift shop
- 면세점 — 15. duty-free shop

수하물 찾기 — D. Baggage Claim

- 수하물 찾는 곳 — 16. baggage claim (area)
- 회전식 수하물 컨베이어 — 17. baggage carousel
- 여행가방 — 18. suitcase
- 휴대용 손수레 — 19. luggage carrier
- 옷가방 — 20. garment bag
- 수하물 — 21. baggage
- 수하물 운반인 — 22. porter/skycap
- 수하물표 — 23. (baggage) claim check

세관 및 출입국 관리소 — E. Customs and Immigration

- 세관 — 24. customs
- 세관원 — 25. customs officer
- 세관 신고서 — 26. customs declaration form
- 출입국 관리소 — 27. immigration
- 이민국 직원 — 28. immigration officer
- 여권 — 29. passport
- 비자 — 30. visa

[1, 2, 4–9, 11–17, 24, 25, 27, 28]

A. Excuse me. Where's the _______?*

B. Right over there.

**With 24 and 27, use:* Excuse me. Where's _______?

[3, 10, 18–21, 23, 26, 29, 30]

A. Oh, no! I think I've lost my _______!

B. I'll help you look for it.

THE AIRPLANE
항공기

조종실	**1.** cockpit	중간 좌석	**17.** middle seat	활주로	**32.** runway
조종사	**2.** pilot/captain	통로쪽 좌석	**18.** aisle seat	터미널	**33.** terminal (building)
부조종사	**3.** co-pilot	좌석벨트 착용신호	**19.** Fasten Seat Belt sign	중앙관제탑	**34.** control tower
계기판	**4.** instrument panel	금연신호	**20.** No Smoking sign	항공기 / 비행기 / 제트여객기	**35.** airplane/plane/jet
항법사	**5.** flight engineer	호출버튼	**21.** call button	기수	**36.** nose
일등실	**6.** first-class section	산소 마스크	**22.** oxygen mask	기체	**37.** fuselage
승객	**7.** passenger	비상출구	**23.** emergency exit	화물칸 문	**38.** cargo door
주방	**8.** galley	팔걸이	**24.** armrest	착륙바퀴	**39.** landing gear
승무원	**9.** flight attendant	좌석등받이 조절버튼	**25.** seat control	날개	**40.** wing
화장실	**10.** lavatory/bathroom	트레이 (테이블)	**26.** tray (table)	엔진	**41.** engine
객실	**11.** cabin	음식	**27.** meal	꼬리날개	**42.** tail
기내 휴대 수화물	**12.** carry-on bag	좌석주머니	**28.** seat pocket	프로펠러 비행기	**43.** propeller plane/prop
기내 수화물칸	**13.** overhead compartment	비상시 행동지침서	**29.** emergency instruction card	프로펠러	**44.** propeller
통로	**14.** aisle	위생봉투	**30.** air sickness bag	헬리콥터	**45.** helicopter
좌석벨트	**15.** seat belt	구명조끼	**31.** life vest	회전익	**46.** rotor (blade)
창가쪽 좌석	**16.** window seat				

A. Where's the _______?
B. In/On/Next to/Behind/In front of/Above/Below the _______.

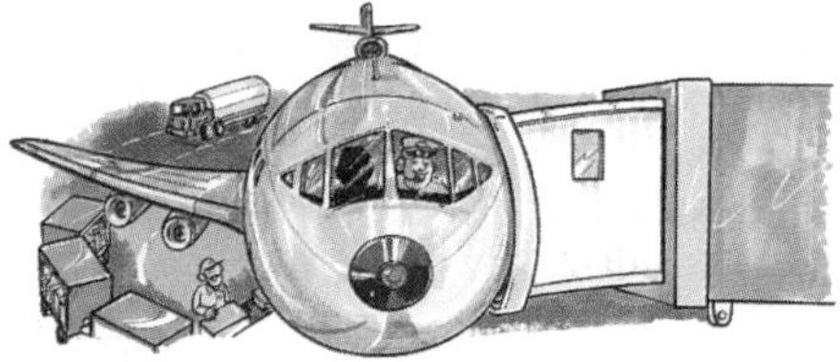

Ladies and gentlemen. This is your captain speaking. I'm sorry for the delay. We had a little problem with one of our _______s.* Everything is fine now and we'll be taking off shortly.

**Use 4, 7, 10, 12, 20–22, 24.*

날씨와 계절

날씨 A. Weather

- 화창한 **1.** sunny
- 구름 낀 **2.** cloudy
- 개인 / 맑은 **3.** clear
- 흐린 **4.** hazy
- 안개가 낀 **5.** foggy
- 바람이 부는 **6.** windy
- 눅눅한 **7.** humid/muggy
- 비가 오는 **8.** raining
- 이슬비가 내리는 **9.** drizzling
- 눈이 내리는 **10.** snowing
- 우박이 내리는 **11.** hailing
- 진눈깨비가 내리는 **12.** sleeting
- 번개 **13.** lightning
- 천둥 **14.** thunderstorm
- 눈보라 **15.** snowstorm
- 태풍 **16.** hurricane/typhoon
- 돌풍 **17.** tornado

온도 B. Temperature

- 온도계 **18.** thermometer
- 화씨 **19.** Fahrenheit
- 섭씨 **20.** Centigrade/Celsius
- 더운 **21.** hot
- 따뜻한 **22.** warm
- 시원한 **23.** cool
- 추운 **24.** cold
- 매우 추운 **25.** freezing

계절 C. Seasons

- 여름 **26.** summer
- 가을 **27.** fall/autumn
- 겨울 **28.** winter
- 봄 **29.** spring

[1–12]
A. What's the weather like?
B. It's ________.

[13–17]
A. What's the weather forecast?
B. There's going to be _[13]_ /a _[14–17]_.

[19–25]
A. How's the weather?
B. It's _[21–25]_.
A. What's the temperature?
B. It's .... degrees _[19, 20]_.

Describe the seasons where you live.
Tell about the weather and the temperature.

What's your favorite season?
Why?

OUTDOOR RECREATION

야외 여가활동

캠핑 / 야영 **A. camping**
- 텐트 / 천막 **1.** tent
- 배낭 **2.** backpack
- 침낭 **3.** sleeping bag
- 말뚝 **4.** tent stakes
- 손도끼 **5.** hatchet
- 랜턴 **6.** lantern
- 캠핑용 스토브 **7.** camp stove

하이킹 **B. hiking**
- 등산화 **8.** hiking boots
- 나침판 **9.** compass
- 지도 **10.** trail map

등산 **C. mountain climbing**
- 등산화 **11.** hiking boots

암벽타기 **D. rock climbing**
- 등산용 밧줄 / 로프 **12.** rope
- 등산장비 **13.** harness

들놀이 / 야유회 **E. picnic**
- 야외 돗자리 **14.** (picnic) blanket
- 보온병 **15.** thermos
- 피크닉 바구니 **16.** picnic basket

[A–E]
A. Let's go ________* this weekend.
B. Good idea! We haven't gone ________* in a long time.

With E, say: on a picnic

[1–16]
A. Did you bring the ________?
B. Yes, I did.

Have you ever gone camping or hiking? Where? What equipment did you use?

Do you like to go on picnics? Where? What picnic supplies and food do you take with you?

THE PARK AND THE PLAYGROUND

공원과 놀이터

- 조깅로 **1.** jogging path
- 화장실 **2.** rest rooms
- 동상 **3.** statue
- 피크닉 장소 **4.** picnic area
- 피크닉 테이블 **5.** picnic table
- 그릴 / 바베큐용 석쇠 **6.** grill
- 쓰레기통 **7.** trash can
- 목마 **8.** merry-go-round/ carousel
- 분수 **9.** fountain
- 동물원 **10.** zoo
- 식수대 **11.** water fountain
- 야외음악당 **12.** band shell
- 승마트랙 **13.** bridle path
- 자전거 세워 두는 곳 **14.** bike rack
- 연못 **15.** duck pond
- 자전거 전용도로 **16.** bicycle path/ bikeway
- 벤치 **17.** bench
- 놀이터 **18.** playground
- 정글짐 **19.** jungle gym
- 구름다리 **20.** monkey bars
- 미끄럼틀 **21.** slide
- 그네 **22.** swings
- 타이어 그네 **23.** tire swing
- 시소 **24.** seesaw
- 어린이 물놀이터 **25.** wading pool
- 모래판 **26.** sandbox
- 모래 **27.** sand

[1–18] A. Excuse me. Does this park have (a) ______?
B. Yes. Right over there.

[19–27] A. { Be careful on the [19–24] !
Be careful in the [25–27] !
B. I will, Mom/Dad.

Describe a park and a playground you are familiar with.

THE BEACH
해수욕장

구조대원	1.	lifeguard
감시대	2.	lifeguard stand
구명구	3.	life preserver
매점	4.	snack bar/ refreshment stand
모래언덕	5.	sand dune
바위	6.	rock
수영하는 사람	7.	swimmer
파도	8.	wave
파도타기하는 사람	9.	surfer
행상인	10.	vendor
일광욕하는 사람	11.	sunbather
모래성	12.	sand castle
조개껍질	13.	seashell/shell
비치 파라솔	14.	beach umbrella
비치의자	15.	(beach) chair
비치타올	16.	(beach) towel
수영복	17.	bathing suit/ swimsuit
수영모자	18.	bathing cap
킥보드	19.	kickboard
서핑보드	20.	surfboard
연	21.	kite
매트리스 튜브 / 공기 매트리스	22.	raft/air mattress
튜브	23.	tube
(비치용) 돗자리	24.	(beach) blanket
차양달린 모자	25.	sun hat
색안경 / 선글라스	26.	sunglasses
선탠로션 / 자외선 차단 로션	27.	suntan lotion/ sunscreen
양동이	28.	pail/bucket
삽	29.	shovel
비치볼	30.	beach ball
아이스박스	31.	cooler

[1–13]
A. What a nice beach!
B. It is. Look at all the ______s!

[14–31]
A. Are you ready for the beach?
B. Almost. I just have to get my ______.

Do you like to go to the beach? Describe your favorite beach. What do you take when you go there?

개인운동 및 여가활동

조깅	**A. jogging**	볼링	**G. bowling**	스쿼시	**L. squash**
조깅복	1. jogging suit	볼링볼	12. bowling ball	스쿼시 라켓	22. squash racquet
조깅화	2. jogging shoes	볼링화	13. bowling shoes	스쿼시 볼	23. squash ball
육상	**B. running**	승마	**H. horseback riding**	핸드볼	**M. handball**
육상복	3. running shorts	안장	14. saddle	핸드볼 장갑	24. handball glove
육상화	4. running shoes	고삐	15. reins	핸드볼	25. handball
		등자꼴의 마구	16. stirrups		
걷기	**C. walking**	스카이다이빙	**I. skydiving**	라켓볼	**N. racquetball**
운동화	5. walking shoes	낙하산	17. parachute	보호안경	26. safety goggles
				라켓볼	27. racquetball
롤러 스케이팅	**D. roller skating**	골프	**J. golf**	라켓	28. racquet
롤러 스케이터	6. roller skates	골프채	18. golf clubs	탁구	**O. ping pong**
무릎 보호대	7. knee pads	골프공	19. golf ball	탁구채	29. paddle
사이클링 / 자전거타기	**E. cycling/ bicycling/biking**	테니스	**K. tennis**	탁구대	30. ping pong table
자전거	8. bicycle/bike	테니스 라켓	20. tennis racquet	네트	31. net
헬멧	9. (bicycle) helmet	테니스공	21. tennis ball	탁구공	32. ping pong ball
스케이트보딩	**F. skateboarding**				
스케이트 보드	10. skateboard				
팔꿈치 보호대	11. elbow pads				

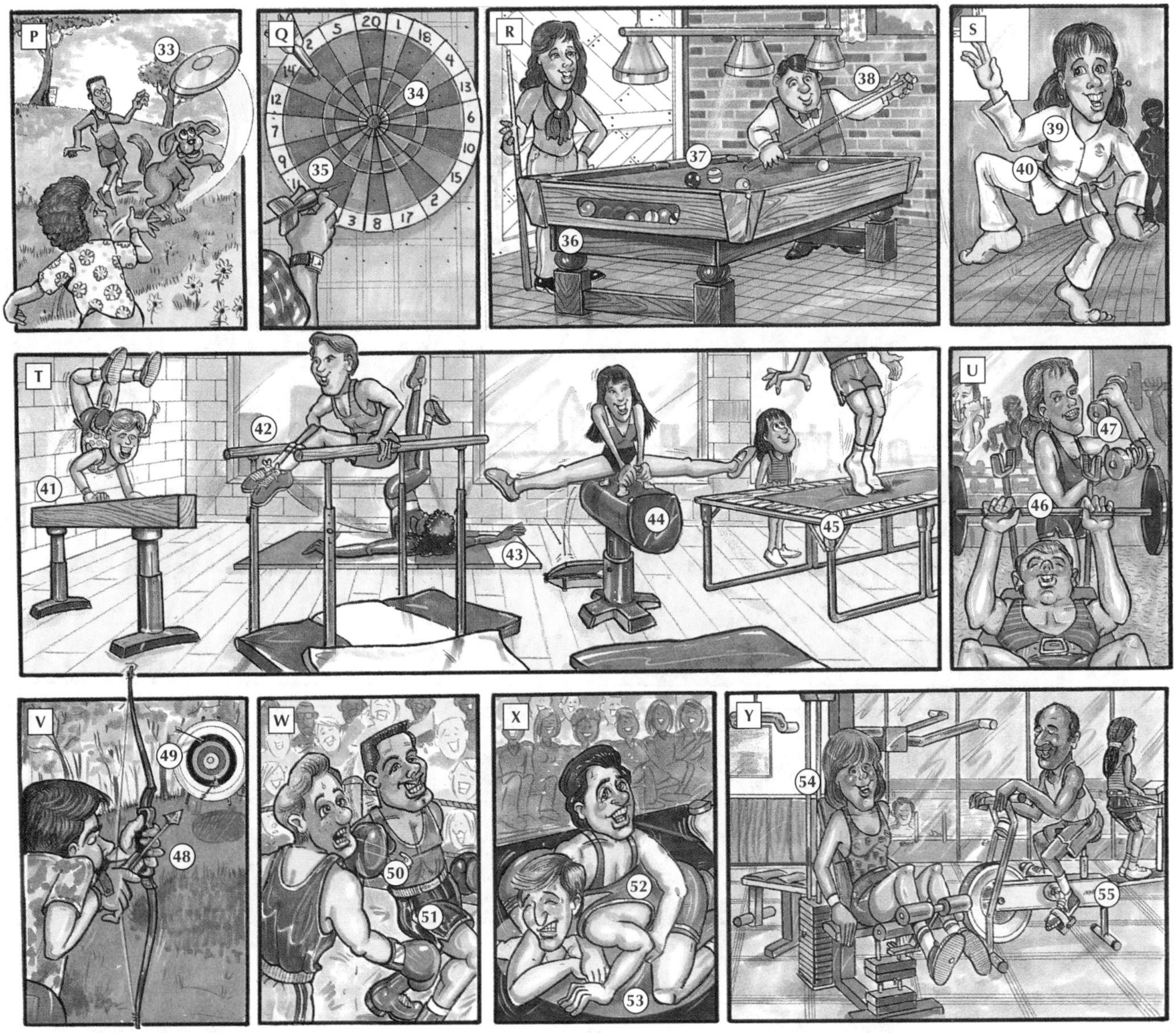

프리스비 **P. frisbee**
프리스비 **33.** frisbee

다트 **Q. darts**
다트보드 **34.** dartboard
다트 **35.** darts

당구 **R. billiards/pool**
당구대 **36.** pool table
당구공 **37.** billiard balls
당구채 **38.** pool stick

가라데 **S. karate**
가라데 복 **39.** karate outfit
가라데 띠 **40.** karate belt

체조 **T. gymnastics**
평행봉 **41.** balance beam
이단 평행봉 **42.** parallel bars
마루 **43.** mat
안마 **44.** horse
트램펄린 **45.** trampoline

역도 **U. weightlifting**
바벨 **46.** barbell
역기 **47.** weights

궁도 **V. archery**
활과 화살 **48.** bow and arrow
표적 **49.** target

권투 **W. box**
권투 글러브 **50.** boxing gloves
복싱팬티 **51.** (boxing) trunks

레슬링 **X. wrestle**
레슬링복 **52.** wrestling uniform
매트 **53.** (wrestling) mat

헬스운동 **Y. work out**
만능운동기구 **54.** universal/exercise equipment
헬스 자전거 **55.** exercise bike

[A–Y]
A. What do you like to do in your free time?
B. I like to go [A–I].
I like to play [J–R].
I like to do [S–V].
I like to [W–Y].

[1–55]
A. I really like this/these new ________.
B. It's/They're very nice.

TEAM SPORTS
단체경기

[A–H]
A. Do you like **baseball**?
B. Yes. **Baseball** is one of my favorite sports.

야구 **A. baseball**
야구선수 1. baseball player
야구장 2. baseball field/ballfield

소프트볼 **B. softball**
소프트볼선수 3. softball player
소프트볼구장 4. ballfield

미식축구 **C. football**
미식축구선수 5. football player
미식축구장 6. football field

라크로스 **D. lacrosse**
라크로스 선수 7. lacrosse player
라크로스 구장 8. lacrosse field

(아이스) 하키 **E. (ice) hockey**
하키선수 9. hockey player
하키링크 10. hockey rink

농구 **F. basketball**
농구선수 11. basketball player
농구장 12. basketball court

배구 **G. volleyball**
배구선수 13. volleyball player
배구장 14. volleyball court

축구 **H. soccer**
축구선수 15. soccer player
축구장 16. soccer field

A. .... plays [A–H] very well.
B. You're right. I think he's/she's one of the best ________s* on the team.

**Use 1, 3, 5, 7, 9, 11, 13, 15.*

A. Now, listen! I want all of you to go out on that ________† and play the best game of [A–H] you've ever played!
B. All right, Coach!

†Use 2, 4, 6, 8, 10, 12, 14, 16.

Which sports on this page do you like to play? Which do you like to watch?
What are your favorite teams?
Name some famous players of these sports.

단체경기 용구

[1–27]
A. I can't find my **baseball**!
B. Look in the *closet*.*

*closet, basement, garage

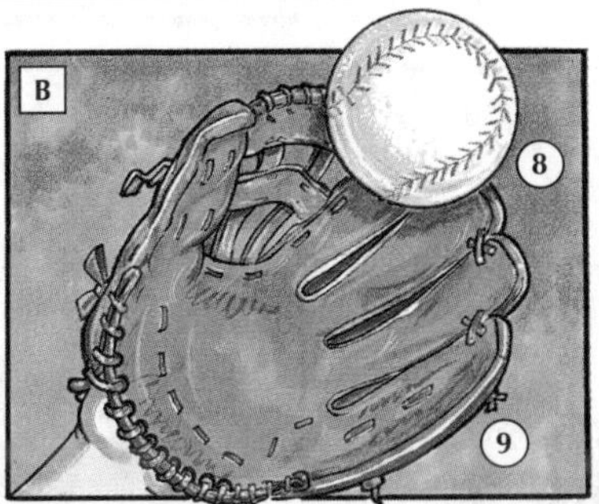

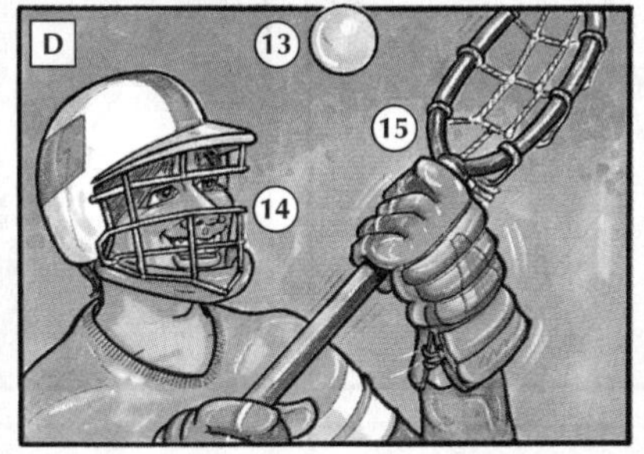

야구 **A. baseball**
야구공 **1.** baseball
방망이 **2.** bat
헬멧 **3.** batting helmet
야구복 **4.** baseball uniform
포수 마스크 **5.** catcher's mask
야구 글러브 **6.** baseball glove
포수 글러브 **7.** catcher's mitt

소프트볼 **B. softball**
소프트볼 **8.** softball
소프트볼 글러브 **9.** softball glove

미식축구 **C. football**
미식축구공 **10.** football
미식축구 헬멧 **11.** football helmet
어깨패드 / 어깨 보호대 **12.** shoulder pads

라크로스 **D. lacrosse**
라크로스볼 **13.** lacrosse ball
얼굴 보호대 **14.** face guard
라크로스 스틱 **15.** lacrosse stick

하키 **E. hockey**
하키퍽 **16.** hockey puck
하키 스틱 **17.** hockey stick
하키 마스크 **18.** hockey mask
하키 글러브 **19.** hockey glove
하키 스케이트 **20.** hockey skates

농구 **F. basketball**
농구공 **21.** basketball
백보드 **22.** backboard
그물망 **23.** basketball hoop

배구 **G. volleyball**
배구공 **24.** volleyball
네트 **25.** volleyball net

축구 **H. soccer**
축구공 **26.** soccer ball
정강이 보호대 **27.** shinguards

[In a store]
A. Excuse me. I'm looking for (a) [1–27].
B. All our [A–H] equipment is over there.
A. Thanks.

[At home]
A. I'm going to play [A–H] after school today.
B. Don't forget your [1–21, 24–27]!

Which sports on this page are popular in your country? Which sports are played in high school?

동계스포츠와 여가활동

[A–H]
A. What's your favorite winter sport?
B. **Skiing**.

(활강) 스키	**A. (downhill) skiing**
스키	1. skis
스키 부츠	2. ski boots
바인딩	3. bindings
폴	4. poles
크로스-컨트리 스키	**B. cross-country skiing**
크로스-컨트리 스키	5. cross-country skis
(아이스) 스케이팅	**C. (ice) skating**
스케이트	6. (ice) skates
스케이트 날집	7. skate guards
피겨 스케이팅	**D. figure skating**
피겨 스케이트	8. figure skates
썰매타기	**E. sledding**
썰매	9. sled
접시모양의 썰매	10. sledding dish/ saucer
봅슬레이 경주	**F. bobsledding**
봅슬레이	11. bobsled
스노우모빌 / 설상차 경주	**G. snowmobiling**
스노우모빌 / 설상차	12. snowmobile
토보건 경주	**H. tobogganing**
토보건	13. toboggan

[A–H]
[At work or at school on Friday]
A. What are you going to do this weekend?
B. I'm going to go ______.

[1–13]
[On the telephone]
A. Hello. Jimmy's Sporting Goods.
B. Hello. Do you sell ______(s)?
A. Yes, we do./No, we don't.

Have you ever watched the Winter Olympics? What is your favorite event? Which event do you think is the most exciting? the most dangerous?

수상 스포츠와 여가활동

[A–L]
A. Would you like to go **sailing** tomorrow?
B. Sure. I'd love to.

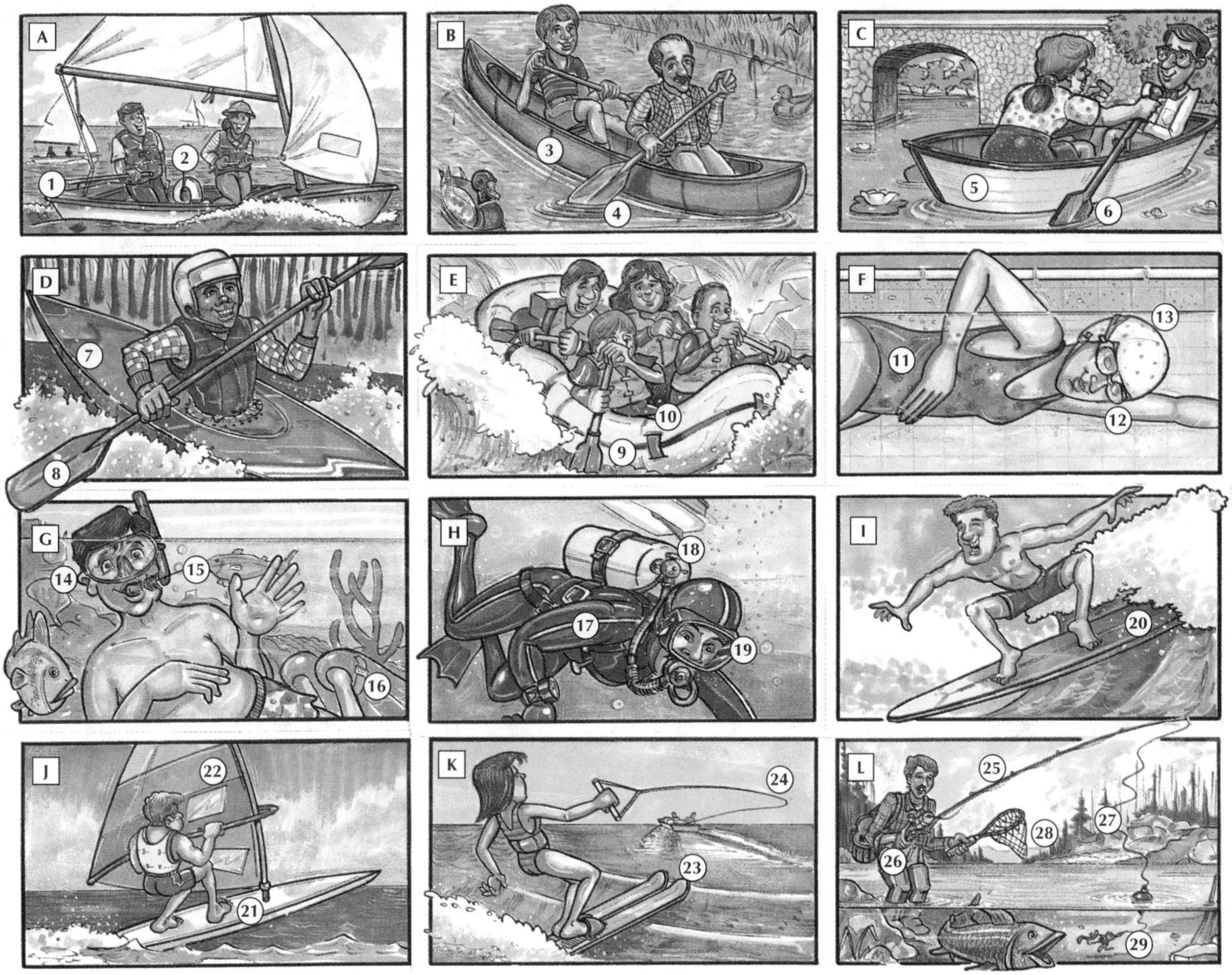

요트타기 A. **sailing**
돛단배 1. sailboat
구명구 2. life preserver

카누경기 B. **canoeing**
카누 3. canoe
노 4. paddles

노젓기 C. **rowing**
노젓는배 5. rowboat
노 6. oars

카약경기 D. **kayaking**
카약 7. kayak
노 8. paddle

뗏목타기 E. **(white water)/rafting**
뗏목 9. raft
구명복 10. life jacket

수영 F. **swimming**
수영복 11. swimsuit/ bathing suit
물안경 12. goggles
수영모 13. bathing cap

잠수 G. **snorkeling**
잠수경 14. mask
잠수용 호흡관 / 스노클 15. snorkel
오리발 16. flippers

스쿠바다이빙 H. **scuba diving**
잠수복 17. wet suit
(산소) 탱크 18. (air) tank
(수중) 마스크 19. (diving) mask

서핑 I. **surfing**
서프 보드 20. surfboard

윈드서핑 J. **windsurfing**
돛달린 서프 보드 / 세일보드 21. sailboard
돛 22. sail

수상스키타기 K. **waterskiing**
수상스키 23. water skis
밧줄 / 로프 24. towrope

낚시 L. **fishing**
낚싯대 25. (fishing) rod
릴 26. reel
낚싯줄 27. (fishing) line
그물 28. net
미끼 29. bait

SPORT AND EXERCISE ACTIONS

운동 / 스포츠동작과 체조동작

치다 **1.** hit
(공을 타자에게) 던지다 **2.** pitch
던지다 **3.** throw
받다 **4.** catch
패스하다 **5.** pass
차다 **6.** kick
서브하다 **7.** serve
튀기다 **8.** bounce
드리블하다 **9.** dribble
슈팅하다 **10.** shoot
뻗다 / 펴다 **11.** stretch
구부리다 **12.** bend

걷다 **13.** walk
달리다 **14.** run
(깡충) 뛰다 **15.** hop
가볍게 뛰다 **16.** skip
뛰어 오르다 **17.** jump
무릎을 꿇다 **18.** kneel
앉다 **19.** sit
눕다 **20.** lie down
뻗치다 **21.** reach
휘두르다 / 흔들다 **22.** swing
밀다 **23.** push
잡아 당기다 **24.** pull

들어 올리다 **25.** lift
수영하다 **26.** swim
다이빙하다 **27.** dive
쏘다 **28.** shoot
팔굽혀 펴기하다 **29.** push-up
윗몸 일으키기하다 **30.** sit-up
누워서 다리 들어올리기를 하다 **31.** leg lift
발뒤꿈치 들어올리기를 하다 **32.** jumping jack
무릎 굽히기를 하다 **33.** deep knee bend
재주넘기를 하다 **34.** somersault
옆으로 재주넘기를 하다 **35.** cartwheel
물구나무서기를 하다 **36.** handstand

[1–10] A. _______ the ball!
B. Okay, Coach!

[11–28] A. Now _______!
B. Like this?
A. Yes.

[29–36] A. Okay, everybody. I want you to do twenty _______s!
B. Twenty _______s?!
A. That's right.

Do you exercise regularly?
Which exercises do you do?

Be an exercise instructor. Lead your friends in an exercise routine using the actions on this page.

수공예, 취미와 놀이

[A–Q]
A. What's your hobby?
B. **Sewing.**

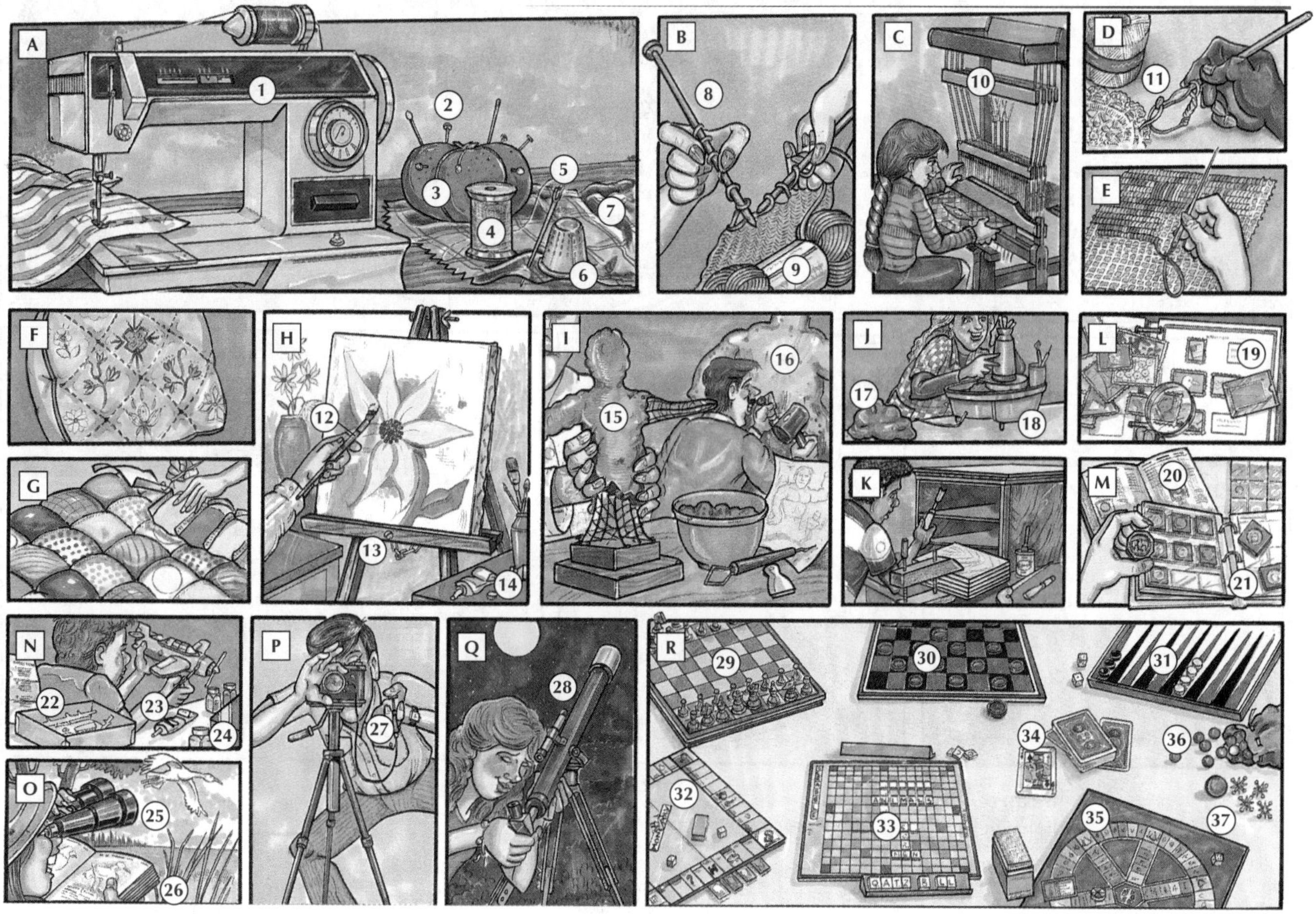

재봉 **A. sewing**
재봉틀 / 미싱 **1.** sewing machine
핀 **2.** pin
바늘꽂이 / 바늘방석 **3.** pin cushion
실 **4.** thread
바늘 **5.** (sewing) needle
골무 **6.** thimble
옷감 **7.** material

뜨개질 **B. knitting**
뜨개질 바늘 **8.** knitting needle
털실 **9.** yarn

직조 **C. weaving**
직기 **10.** loom

레이스 뜨기 **D. crocheting**
코바늘 **11.** crochet hook

바늘로 뜨는 레이스 **E. needlepoint**

수놓기 **F. embroidery**

퀼팅 / 조각이불 만들기 **G. quilting**

그림그리기 **H. painting**
붓 **12.** paintbrush
이젤 **13.** easel
물감 **14.** paint

조각 **I. sculpting/sculpture**
석고 **15.** plaster
돌 **16.** stone

도기만들기 **J. pottery**
점토 **17.** clay
물레 **18.** potter's wheel

목공예 **K. woodworking**

우표수집 **L. stamp collecting**
우표 앨범 **19.** stamp album

동전수집 **M. coin collecting**
동전 카탈로그 **20.** coin catalog
동전 수집용 앨범 **21.** coin album

모형만들기 **N. model building**
모형조립세트 **22.** model kit
접착제 **23.** (model) glue
물감 **24.** (model) paint

조류 관찰 **O. bird watching**
쌍안경 **25.** binoculars
안내서 **26.** field guide

사진찍기 **P. photography**
사진기 **27.** camera

천체 관측 **Q. astronomy**
망원경 **28.** telescope

게임 **R. games**
서양장기 **29.** chess
체커 **30.** checkers
서양 주사위놀이 **31.** backgammon
모노폴리 **32.** Monopoly
스크래블 **33.** Scrabble
카드 **34.** cards
트리비얼 퍼슈트 **35.** Trivial Pursuit
구슬치기 **36.** marbles
잭 **37.** jacks

[1–28] [In a store]
A. May I help you?
B. Yes, please. I'd like to buy (a/an) ______.

[29–37] [At home]
A. What do you want to do?
B. Let's play ______.

What's your hobby?
What games are popular in your country? Describe how to play one.

공연

극장 **A. theater**
- 조명 **1.** lights/lighting
- 커튼 **2.** curtain
- 스포트 라이트 **3.** spotlight
- 배경 **4.** scenery
- 무대 **5.** stage
- 합창단 **6.** chorus
- 무용수 **7.** dancer
- 여자배우 **8.** actress
- 남자배우 **9.** actor
- 관현악단 / 오케스트 라 **10.** orchestra
- 오케스트 라 연주석 **11.** orchestra pit
- 관객 **12.** audience
- 통로 **13.** aisle
- 1층 관람석 **14.** orchestra
- 2층 관람석 **15.** mezzanine
- 3층 관람석 / 발코니 **16.** balcony
- 안내원 **17.** usher
- 프로그램 **18.** program
- 관람표 **19.** ticket

교향악 **B. symphony**
- 교향악단 **20.** symphony orchestra
- 연주자 **21.** musician
- 지휘자 **22.** conductor
- 지휘봉 **23.** baton
- 지휘대 **24.** podium

오페라 **C. opera**
- 오페라 가수 **25.** opera singer
- 오페라단 **26.** opera company

발레 **D. ballet**
- 무용수 **27.** ballet dancer
- 여자무용수 / 발레리나 **28.** ballerina
- 발레단 **29.** ballet company
- 발레화 **30.** ballet slippers
- 토우슈즈 **31.** toeshoes

영화 **E. movies**
- (극장입구에 돌출한) 차양 **32.** marquee
- 매표소 **33.** box office
- 게시판 **34.** billboard
- 로비 **35.** lobby
- 매점 **36.** refreshment stand
- 화면 **37.** (movie) screen

[A–E]
A. What are you doing this evening?
B. I'm going to the ________.

[1–11, 20–37]
A. { What a magnificent ________!
   { What magnificent ________s!
B. I agree.

[14–16]
A. Where did you sit during the performance?
B. We sat in the ________.

What kinds of entertainment on this page are popular in your country?

Tell about a play, concert, opera, ballet, or movie you have seen. Describe the performance and the theater.

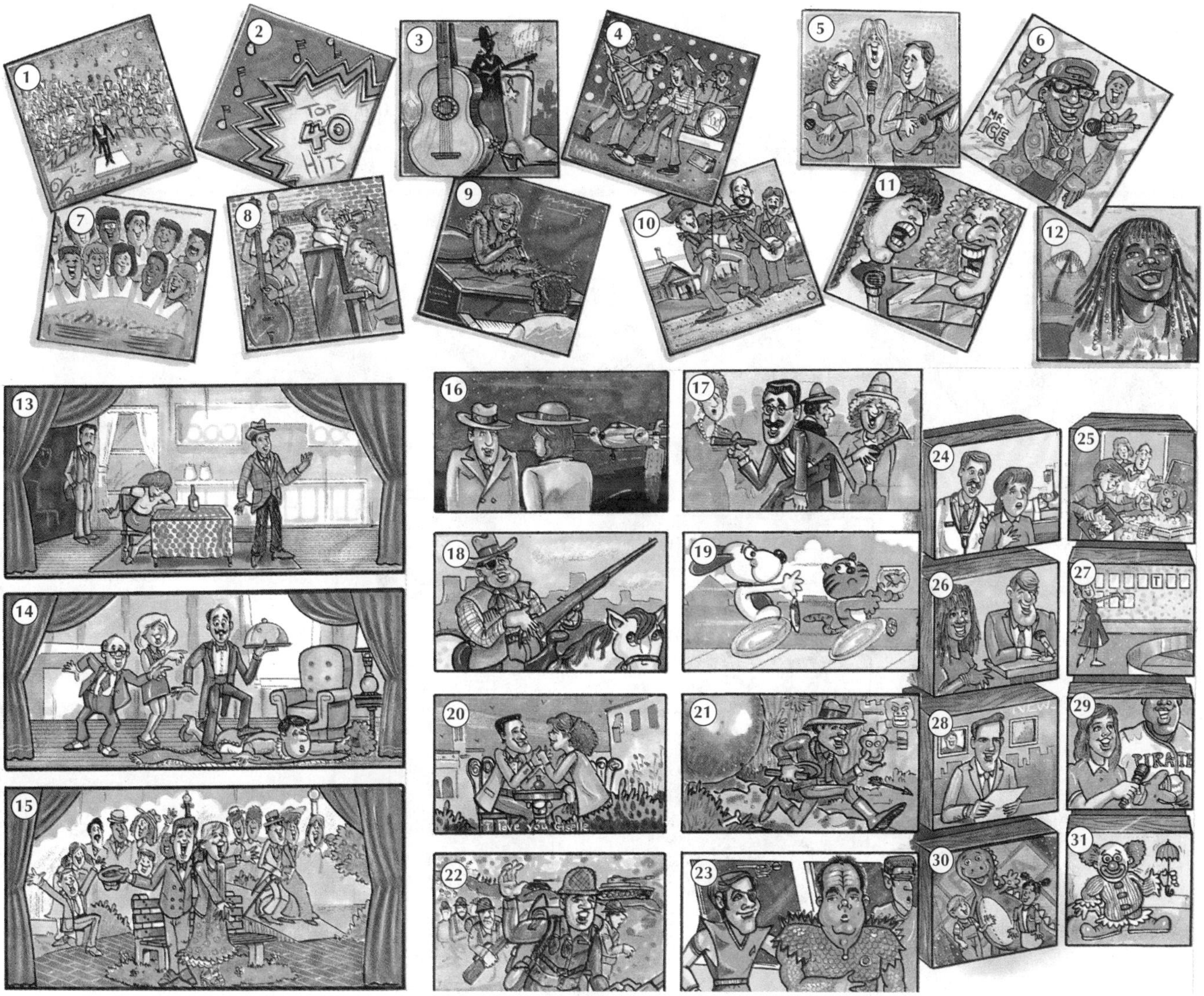

TYPES OF ENTERTAINMENT
공연의 종류

	A. music		**B. plays**		**D. TV programs**
음악		연극		텔레비전 프로그램	
고전음악	1. classical music	드라마	13. drama	드라마	24. drama
대중음악	2. popular music	코메디	14. comedy	시츄에이션 코메디 / 시트콤	25. (situation) comedy/ sitcom
컨츄리음악	3. country music	뮤지컬(코메디)	15. musical (comedy)	대담프로	26. talk show
록음악	4. rock music	영화	**C. movies**	오락프로	27. game show
민요	5. folk music	드라마	16. drama	뉴스프로	28. news program
랩음악	6. rap music	코메디	17. comedy	스포츠프로	29. sports program
복음 싱가	7. gospel music	서부영화	18. western	어린이프로	30. children's program
재즈	8. jazz	만화영화	19. cartoon	만화영화	31. cartoon
부르스	9. blues	외국영화	20. foreign film		
블루그래스	10. bluegrass	모험영화	21. adventure movie		
헤비메탈	11. heavy metal	전쟁영화	22. war movie		
레게음악	12. reggae	공상과학영화	23. science fiction movie		

A. What kind of [A–D] do you like?

B. I like [1–12].
I like [13–31]s.

What's your favorite type of music?
Who is your favorite singer? musician? musical group?

What kind of movies do you like?
Who are your favorite movie stars?
What are the titles of your favorite movies?

What kind of TV programs do you like?
What are your favorite shows?

MUSICAL INSTRUMENTS
악기

A. Do you play a musical instrument?
B. Yes. I play the **violin**.

현악기 A. Strings
- 바이올린 **1.** violin
- 비올라 **2.** viola
- 첼로 **3.** cello
- 바스 **4.** bass
- 기타 **5.** (acoustic) guitar
- 우쿨렐레 **6.** ukelele
- 전자기타 **7.** electric guitar
- 밴조 **8.** banjo
- 만돌린 **9.** mandolin
- 하프 **10.** harp

목관악기 B. Woodwinds
- 피콜로 **11.** piccolo
- 플루트 **12.** flute
- 클라리넷 **13.** clarinet
- 오보엣 **14.** oboe
- 리코더 **15.** recorder
- 색소폰 **16.** saxophone
- 바순 / 파곳 **17.** bassoon

금관악기 C. Brass
- 트럼펫 **18.** trumpet
- 트럼본 **19.** trombone
- 프렌치 혼 **20.** French horn
- 튜바 **21.** tuba

타악기 D. Percussion
- 드럼 **22.** drum
- 케틀드럼 **23.** kettle drum
- 봉고 **24.** bongos
- 콩가(드럼) **25.** conga (drum)
- 심벌즈 **26.** cymbals
- 실로폰 **27.** xylophone

건반악기 E. Keyboard Instruments
- 피아노 **28.** piano
- 오르간 **29.** organ
- 전자피아노 / 디지털 피아노 **30.** electric piano/ digital piano
- 신시사이저 **31.** synthesizer

기타악기 F. Other Instruments
- 아코디언 **32.** accordion
- 하모니카 **33.** harmonica

A. You play the ______ very well.
B. Thank you.

A. What's that noise?
B. That's my son/daughter practicing the ______.

Do you play a musical instrument? Which one?
Name and describe other musical instruments used in your country.

나무, 꽃 및 화초

나무 **1.** tree
나뭇잎 **2.** leaf–leaves
잔가지 **3.** twig
가지 **4.** branch
큰가지 **5.** limb
줄기 **6.** trunk
나무껍질 **7.** bark
뿌리 **8.** root
솔잎 **9.** needle
솔방울 **10.** cone
층층나무 **11.** dogwood
호랑가시 나무 / 감 탕나무 **12.** holly
목련 **13.** magnolia
느릅나무 **14.** elm
벚나무 **15.** cherry
야자수 **16.** palm
자작나무 **17.** birch
단풍나무 **18.** maple
참나무 **19.** oak
소나무 **20.** pine
미국 삼나무 **21.** redwood
버드나무 **22.** (weeping) willow
꽃 **23.** flower
꽃잎 **24.** petal
암술 **25.** pistula
수술 **26.** stamen
줄기 **27.** stem
꽃봉오리 **28.** bud
가시 **29.** thorn
구근 **30.** bulb
국화 **31.** chrysanthemum/mum
나팔수선화 **32.** daffodil
데이지 **33.** daisy
치자나무 **34.** gardenia
백합 **35.** lily
팬지 **36.** pansy
피튜니아 **37.** petunia
난초 **38.** orchid
장미 **39.** rose
해바라기 **40.** sunflower
튤립 **41.** tulip
제비꽃 **42.** violet
덤불 **43.** bush
관목 **44.** shrub
양치 **45.** fern
화초 **46.** plant
선인장 **47.** cactus–cacti
덩굴 **48.** vine
잔디 / 풀 **49.** grass
덩굴 옻나무 **50.** poison ivy

[11–22]
A. What kind of tree is that?
B. I think it's a/an _______ tree.

[31–48]
A. Look at all the _______s!
B. They're beautiful!

Describe your favorite tree and your favorite flower.
What kinds of trees and flowers grow where you live?

In your country, are flowers used at weddings? at funerals? on holidays? on visits to the hospital? Tell which flowers are used for different occasions.

THE ENVIRONMENT AND ENERGY
환경과 에너지

삼림 / 숲	**1.** forest/woods	절벽	**13.** cliff	산성비	**25.** acid rain
호수	**2.** lake	협곡	**14.** canyon	독성폐기물	**26.** toxic waste
초원	**3.** meadow	강	**15.** river	방사선	**27.** radiation
산	**4.** mountain	댐	**16.** dam	수질오염	**28.** water pollution
계곡	**5.** valley	사막	**17.** desert	석유	**29.** oil
폭포	**6.** waterfall	모래언덕	**18.** dune	(천연)가스	**30.** (natural) gas
여울	**7.** rapids	밀림	**19.** jungle	석탄	**31.** coal
언덕	**8.** hill	해변	**20.** seashore	바람	**32.** wind
들판	**9.** field	만	**21.** bay	원자력에너지 / 핵에너지	**33.** nuclear energy
시내	**10.** stream/brook	대양	**22.** ocean	태양에너지	**34.** solar energy
연못	**11.** pond	섬	**23.** island	수력	**35.** hydroelectric power
평원	**12.** plateau	공기오염	**24.** air pollution		

[1–23] A. { Isn't this a beautiful ________?!
Aren't these beautiful ________?!
B. It's/They're magnificent.

[24–28] A. Do you worry about the environment?
B. Yes. I'm very concerned about ________.

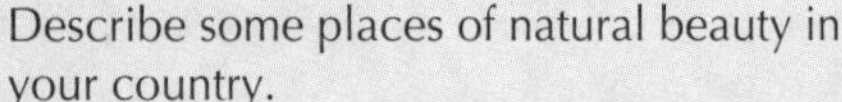

Describe some places of natural beauty in your country.

What kind of energy do you use to heat your home? to cook?
In your opinion, which kind of energy is best for producing electricity?

THE FARM AND FARM ANIMALS
농장과 가축

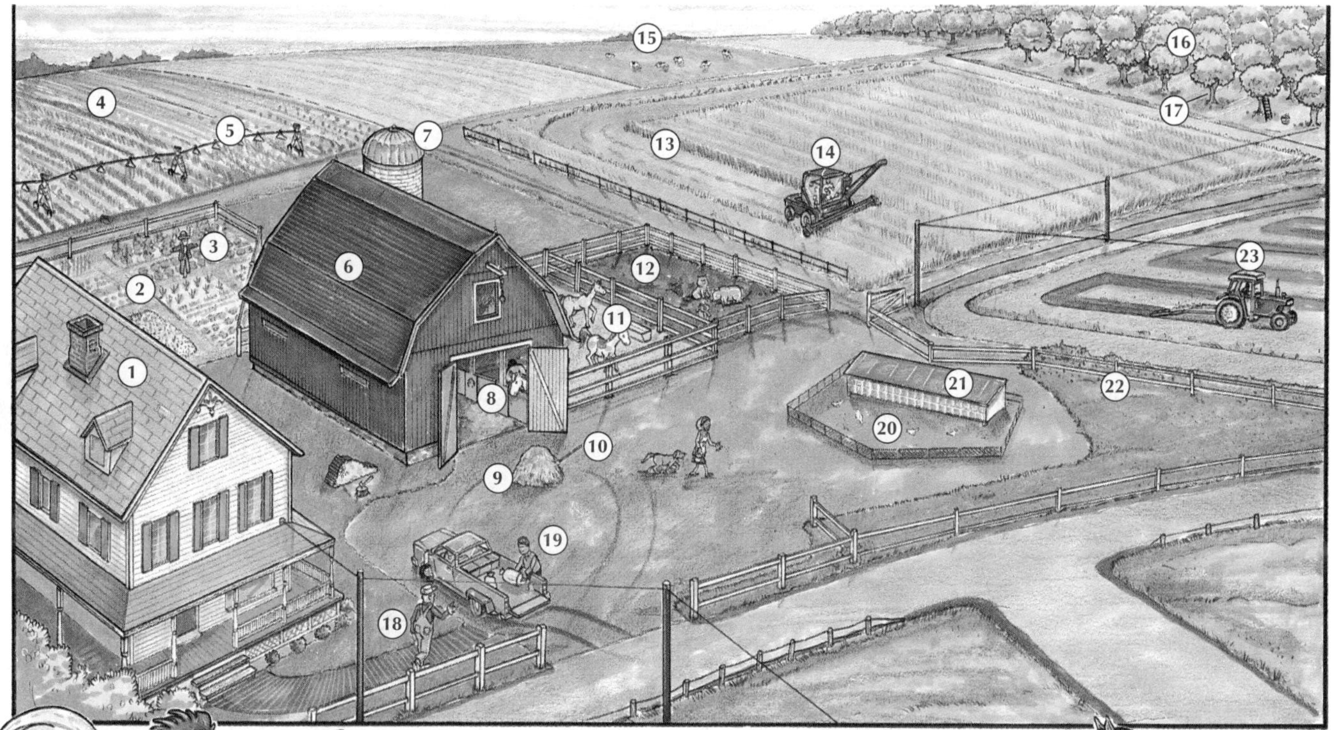

농가	**1.** farmhouse	콤바인	**14.** combine	칠면조	**27.** turkey
텃밭	**2.** (vegetable) garden	목초지	**15.** pasture	염소	**28.** goat
허수아비	**3.** scarecrow	과수원	**16.** orchard	염소새끼	**29.** kid
농작물	**4.** crop	과수	**17.** fruit tree	양	**30.** sheep
관개시설	**5.** irrigation system	농부	**18.** farmer	어린양	**31.** lamb
헛간	**6.** barn	품꾼	**19.** hired hand	황소	**32.** bull
사일로	**7.** silo	닭우리	**20.** chicken coop	젖소	**33.** (dairy) cow
외양간 / 마구간	**8.** stable	닭장	**21.** hen house	송아지	**34.** calf–calves
건초	**9.** hay	울타리	**22.** fence	말	**35.** horse
쇠스랑	**10.** pitchfork	트랙터	**23.** tractor	돼지	**36.** pig
헛간의 앞뜰	**11.** barnyard	수탉	**24.** rooster	돼지새끼	**37.** piglet
돼지우리	**12.** pig pen/pig sty	암탉	**25.** chicken/hen		
밭 / 논	**13.** field	병아리	**26.** chick		

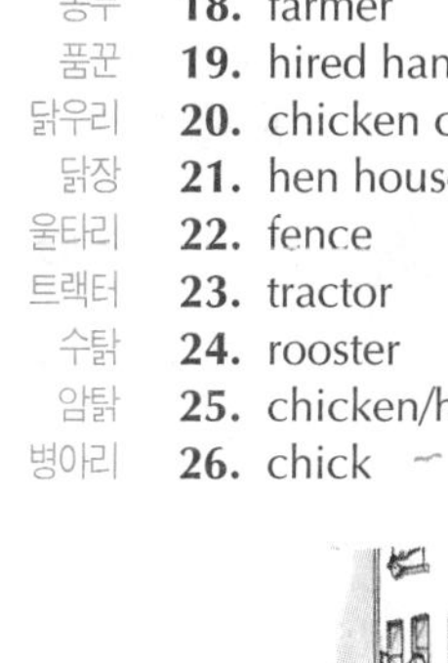

A. Where's the ________?
B. In/On/Next to the ________.

A. The [24–37] s got loose again!
B. Oh, no! Where are they?
A. They're in the [1, 2, 12, 13, 15, 16, 20, 21]!

Tell about farms in your country.
What crops and animals are common on these farms?

야생동물과 애완동물

여우 **1.** fox
고슴도치 **2.** porcupine
바 늘 **a.** quill
너구리 **3.** raccoon
늑대 **4.** wolf–wolves
무스 **5.** moose
뿔 **a.** antler
사슴 **6.** deer
발굽 **a.** hoof
아기사슴 **7.** fawn
생쥐 **8.** mouse–mice
칩멍크 **9.** chipmunk
쥐 **10.** rat
다람쥐 **11.** squirrel
토끼 **12.** rabbit
땅다람쥐 **13.** gopher
비버 **14.** beaver

박쥐 **15.** bat
스컹크 **16.** skunk
주머니쥐 **17.** possum
당나귀 **18.** donkey
버팔로 / 큰 들소 **19.** buffalo
낙타 **20.** camel
혹 **a.** hump
라마 **21.** llama
말 **22.** horse
꼬리 **a.** tail
망아지 **23.** foal
조랑말 **24.** pony
아르마딜로 **25.** armadillo
캥거루 **26.** kangaroo
육아주머니 **a.** pouch
표범 **27.** leopard
넨점 **a.** spots

기린 **28.** giraffe
들소 **29.** bison
코끼리 **30.** elephant
상아 / 엄니 **a.** tusk
코 **b.** trunk
호랑이 **31.** tiger
발톱 **a.** paw
사자 **32.** lion
갈기 **a.** mane
하마 **33.** hippopotamus
하이에나 **34.** hyena
코뿔소 **35.** rhinoceros
뿔 **a.** horn
얼룩말 **36.** zebra
줄무늬 **a.** stripes

흑곰 **37.** black bear
발톱 **a.** claw
회갈색곰 **38.** grizzly bear
북극곰 **39.** polar bear
코알라 **40.** koala (bear)
팬더 **41.** panda
원숭이 **42.** monkey
침팬지 **43.** chimpanzee

긴팔원숭이 **44.** gibbon
비비 **45.** baboon
오랑우탄 **46.** orangutan
고릴라 **47.** gorilla
개미핥기 **48.** anteater
지렁이 **49.** worm
민달팽이 **50.** slug

애완동물 Pets
고양이 **51.** cat
수염 **a.** whiskers
새끼고양이 **52.** kitten
개 **53.** dog
강아지 **54.** puppy
햄스터 **55.** hamster
게르빌루스쥐 **56.** gerbil
기니아픽 **57.** guinea pig

[1–50] A. Look at that ______!
B. Wow! That's the biggest ______ I've ever seen!

[51–57] A. Do you have a pet?
B. Yes. I have a ______.
A. What's your ______'s name?
B. …………

What animals can be found where you live?
Is there a zoo near where you live? What animals does the zoo have?
What are some common pets in your country?
If you were an animal, which animal do you think you would be? Why?
Does your culture have any popular folk tales or children's stories about animals? Tell a story you are familiar with.

BIRDS AND INSECTS
조류와 곤충

조류	**A. Birds**
울새	**1.** robin
둥지	**a.** nest
알	**b.** egg
북미산 어치 / 아메리카 어치	**2.** blue jay
날개	**a.** wing
꼬리	**b.** tail
깃털	**c.** feather
홍관조	**3.** cardinal
벌새	**4.** hummingbird
꿩	**5.** pheasant
까마귀	**6.** crow
갈매기	**7.** seagull
참새	**8.** sparrow
딱따구리	**9.** woodpecker
부리	**a.** beak
제비	**10.** swallow
비둘기	**11.** pigeon
부엉이	**12.** owl
매	**13.** hawk
독수리	**14.** eagle
발톱	**a.** claw
카나리아	**15.** canary
카커투 / 도가머리앵무새	**16.** cockatoo
앵무새	**17.** parrot
잉꼬	**18.** parakeet
오리	**19.** duck
부리	**a.** bill
새끼오리	**20.** duckling
거위	**21.** goose
백조	**22.** swan
홍학	**23.** flamingo
두루미	**24.** crane
황새	**25.** stork
펠리컨	**26.** pelican
공작	**27.** peacock
펭귄	**28.** penguin
뻐꾸기	**29.** roadrunner
타조	**30.** ostrich

곤충류	**B. Insects**
파리	**31.** fly
모기	**32.** mosquito
벼룩	**33.** flea
개똥벌레	**34.** firefly/ lightning bug
나방	**35.** moth
잠자리	**36.** dragonfly
거미	**37.** spider
거미줄	**a.** web
무당벌레	**38.** ladybug
말벌	**39.** wasp
진드기	**40.** tick
벌	**41.** bee
벌집	**a.** beehive
애벌레	**42.** caterpillar
고치	**a.** cocoon
나비	**43.** butterfly
메뚜기	**44.** grasshopper
개미	**45.** ant
딱정벌레	**46.** beetle
흰개미	**47.** termite
바퀴벌레	**48.** roach/ cockroach
전갈	**49.** scorpion
지네	**50.** centipede
사마귀	**51.** praying mantis
귀뚜라미	**52.** cricket

[1–52] A. Is that a/an _______?
B. No. I think it's a/an _______.

[31–52] A. Hold still! There's a _______ on your shirt!
B. Oh! Can you get it off of me?
A. There! It's gone!

What birds and insects can be found where you live?

Does your culture have any popular folk tales or children's stories about birds or insects? Tell a story you are familiar with.

FISH, SEA ANIMALS, AND REPTILES
물고기, 바다동물 및 파충류

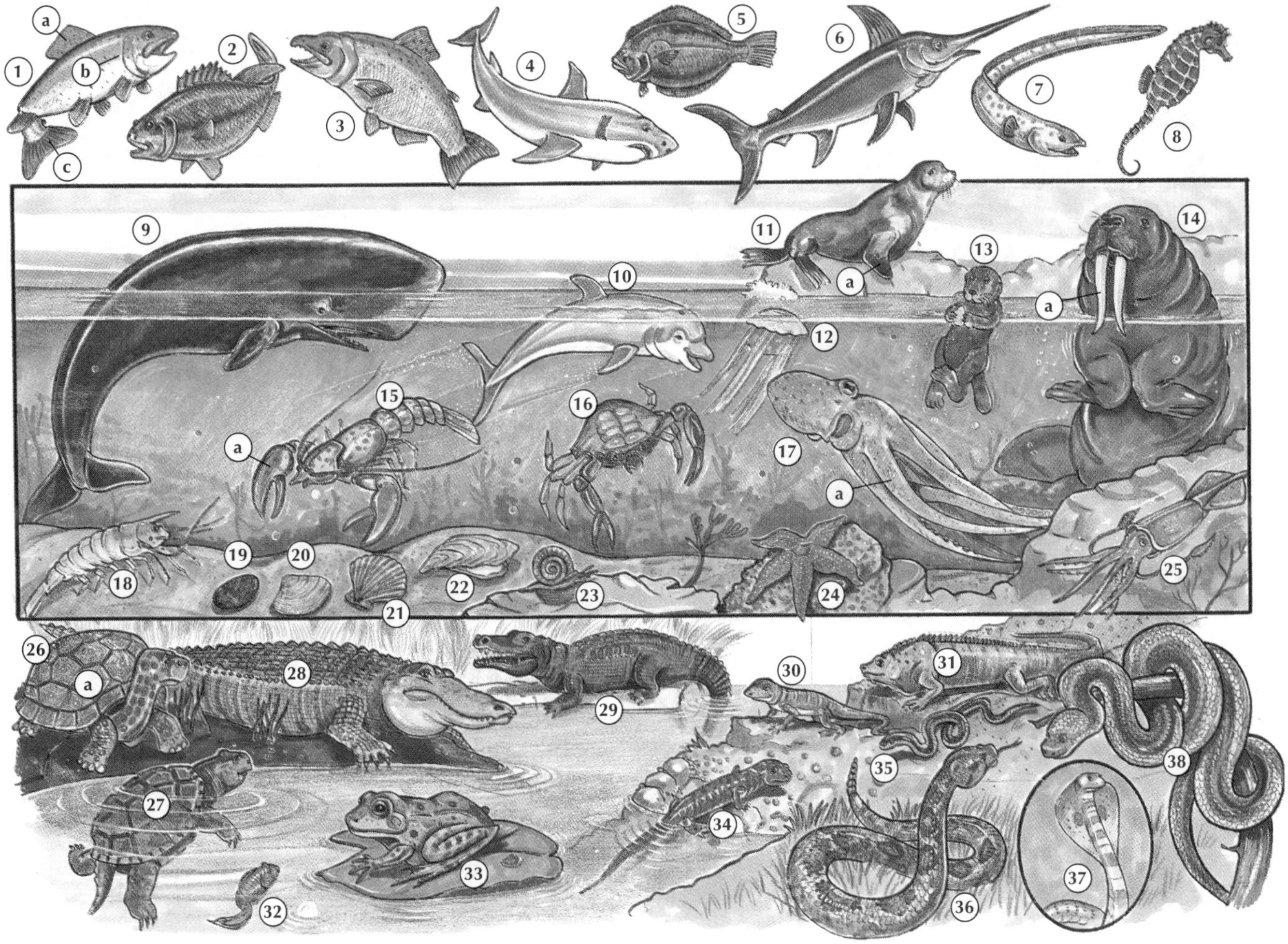

A. Fish (물고기)
1. trout 송어
   a. fin 지느러미
   b. gill 아가미
   c. tail 꼬리
2. bass 농어
3. salmon 연어
4. shark 상어
5. flounder 가자미 / 도다리
6. swordfish 황새치
7. eel 뱀장어
8. sea horse 해마

B. Sea Animals (바다동물)
9. whale 고래
10. dolphin 돌고래
11. seal 바다표범
    a. flipper 지느러미 발
12. jellyfish 해파리
13. otter 수달
14. walrus 바다코끼리
    a. tusk 엄니
15. lobster 가재
    a. claw 집게발
16. crab 게
17. octopus 문어
    a. tentacle 촉수
18. shrimp 새우
19. mussel 홍합
20. clam 대합
21. scallop 가리비 / 스캘롭
22. oyster 굴
23. snail 달팽이
24. starfish 불가사리
25. squid 오징어

C. Amphibians and Reptiles (양서류와 파충류)
26. tortoise (육지) 거북이
    a. shell 등
27. turtle (바다) 거북이
28. alligator 악어
29. crocodile 악어
30. lizard 도마뱀
31. iguana 이구아나
32. tadpole 올챙이
33. frog 개구리
34. salamander 도롱뇽
35. snake 뱀
36. rattlesnake 방울뱀
37. cobra 코브라
38. boa constrictor 왕뱀 / 브라질 보아

[1–38] A. Is that a/an _______?
B. No. I think it's a/an _______.

[26–38] A. Are there any _______s around here?
B. No. But there are lots of _______s.

What fish, sea animals, and reptiles can be found in your country? Which ones are endangered and need to be protected? Why?

In your opinion, which ones are the most interesting? the most beautiful? the most dangerous?

계측과 기하도형

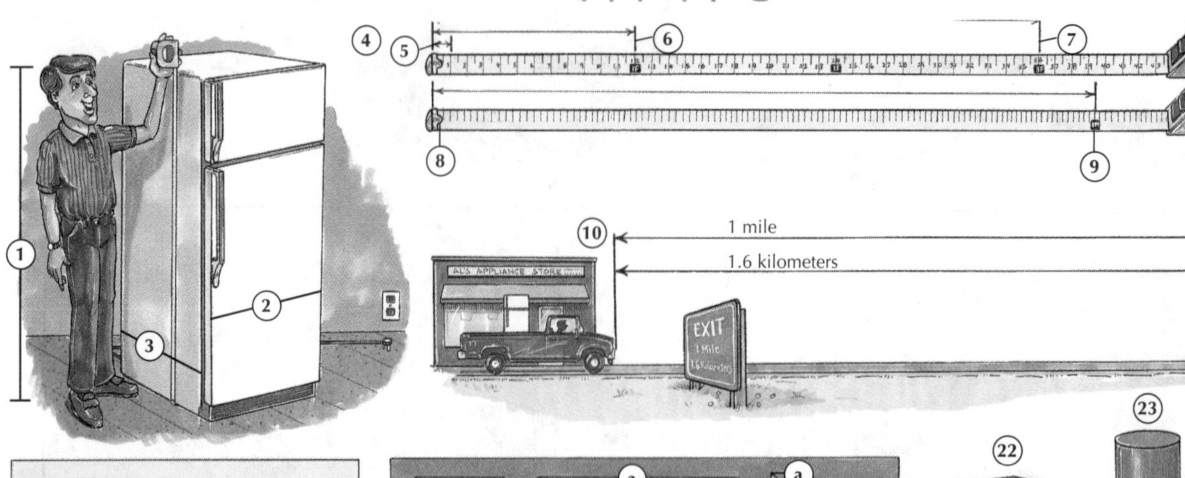

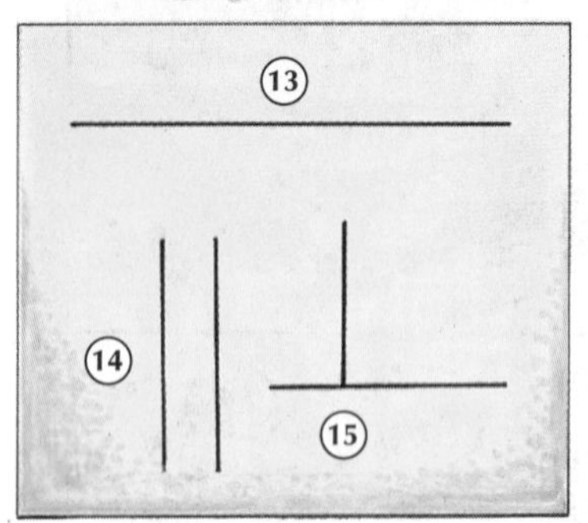

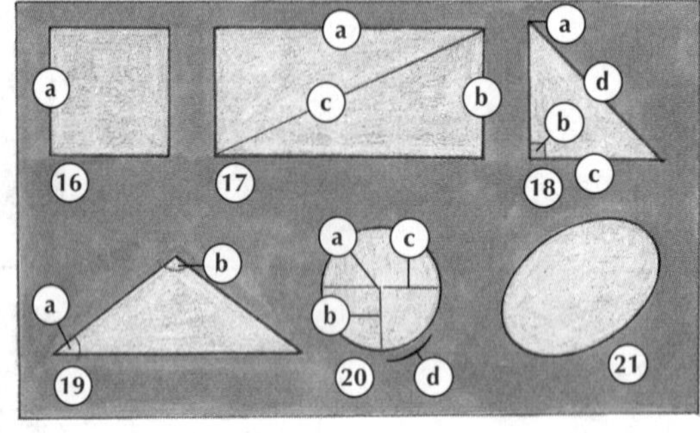

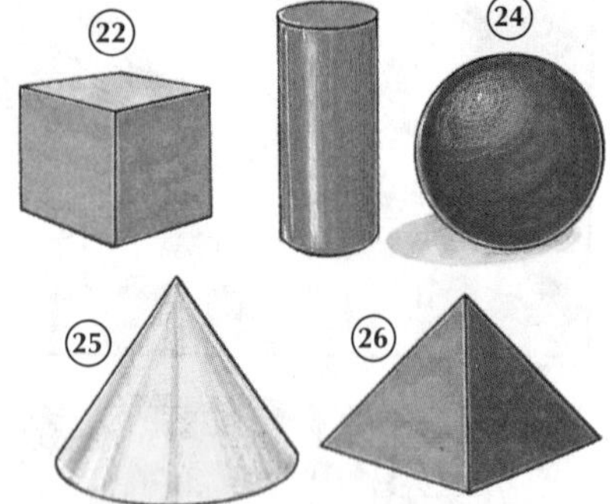

A. Measurements 계측
1. height 높이
2. width 넓이
3. depth 깊이
4. length 길이
5. inch 인치
6. foot–feet 피트
7. yard 야드
8. centimeter 센티미터
9. meter 미터
10. distance 거리
11. mile 마일
12. kilometer 킬로미터

B. Lines 선
13. straight line 직선
14. parallel lines 평행선
15. perpendicular lines 수직선

C. Geometric Shapes 기하도형
16. square 정사각형
    a. side 면
17. rectangle 직사각형
    a. length 세로
    b. width 가로
    c. diagonal 대각선
18. right triangle 직각삼각형
    a. apex 꼭지점
    b. right angle 직각
    c. base 밑변
    d. hypotenuse 빗변
19. isosceles triangle 이등변삼각형
    a. acute angle 예각
    b. obtuse angle 둔각
20. circle 원
    a. center 중심
    b. radius 반지름
    c. diameter 지름
    d. circumference 원주
21. ellipse/oval 타원

D. Solid Figures 입체도형
22. cube 입방체
23. cylinder 원기둥
24. sphere 구
25. cone 원추
26. pyramid 피라밋 / 각뿔

[1–9]
A. What's the [1–4] ?
B. .... [5–9] (s).

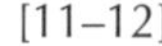

[11–12]
A. What's the distance?
B. .... ______(s).

1 inch (1")	=	2.54 centimeters (cm)
1 foot (1')	=	0.305 meters (m)
1 yard (1 yd.)	=	0.914 meters (m)
1 mile (mi.)	=	1.6 kilometers (km)

[16–21]
A. Who can tell me what shape this is?
B. I can. It's a/an ______.

[22–26]
A. Who knows what figure this is?
B. I do. It's a/an ______.

[13–26]
A. This painting is magnificent!
B. Hmm. I don't think so. It just looks like a lot of ______s and ______s to me!

우주와 우주탐험

우주 A. The Universe

은하수 / 성운 **1.** galaxy
별 / 항성 **2.** star
별자리 / 성좌 **3.** constellation
큰 곰자리 / 북두칠성 **a.** The Big Dipper
작은 곰자리 **b.** The Little Dipper

태양계 B. The Solar System

태양 **4.** sun
달 **5.** moon
행성 / 혹성 **6.** planet
월식 **7.** solar eclipse
일식 **8.** lunar eclipse
유성 / 운석 **9.** meteor
혜성 **10.** comet
소행성 **11.** asteroid
수성 **12.** Mercury
금성 **13.** Venus
지구 **14.** Earth
화성 **15.** Mars
목성 **16.** Jupiter
토성 **17.** Saturn
천왕성 **18.** Uranus
혜왕성 **19.** Neptune
명왕성 **20.** Pluto

우주탐험 C. Space Exploration

인공위성 **21.** satellite
우주탐색기 **22.** (space) probe

우주선 **23.** space craft/orbiter
우주 정거장 **24.** space station
우주 비행사 **25.** astronaut
우주복 **26.** space suit
로켓 **27.** rocket
발사대 **28.** launch pad
우주 왕복선 **29.** space shuttle
추진 로케트 **30.** booster rocket
우주 관제센터 **31.** mission control
유에프오 / 미확인 비행물체 **32.** U.F.O./ Unidentified/ Flying Object/ flying saucer

[1–20]
A. Is that (a/an/the) ________?
B. I'm not sure. I think it might be (a/an/the) ________.

[21–27, 29, 31]
A. Is the ________ ready for tomorrow's launch?
B. Yes. "All systems are go!"

Pretend you are an astronaut traveling in space. What do you see?
Draw and name a constellation you are familiar with.

Do you think space exploration is important? Why?
Have you ever seen a U.F.O.? Do you believe there is life in outer space? Why?

어휘목록

굵은 활자의 숫자는 단어의 페이지를 가리키며, 그 다음에 나오는 숫자는 그 페이지 안에서의 단어의 위치를 가리킨다. 예를 들어, north 5-1"의 경우, 5페이지에 단어 north가 나오며, 이 단어의 항목은 1번이다.

가 **1**-7
가구 광택제 **24**-26
가구점 **35**-24
가구코너 **62**-14
가금류 **47**-F
가난한 **40**-50
가득찬 **40**-59
가라데 **103**-S
가라데 띠 **103**-43
가라데 복 **103**-39
가려운 **71**-50
가로 **120**-17-b
가로등 **38**-6
가로등 기둥 **25**-1
가르치다 **85**-24
가리비 **47**-64 **119**-21
가벼운 **40**-12 **61**-12
가볍게 뛰다 **108**-16
가스 **114**-30
가스 레인지 **18**-19
가스요금 청구서 **27**-12
가슴 **68**-29
가시 **113**-29
가운뎃손가락 **69**-47
가위 **23**-13 **88**-27
가을 **98**-27
가자미 **47**-59 **119**-5
가재 **119**-15
가전제품 수리공 **27**-5
가전제품 코너 **62**-15
가전제품 판매점 **34**-1
가정부 **81**-29
가정용품 **29** **49**-H
가정학 **78**-15
가제 **72**-24
가족구성원 **2** **3**
가죽잠바 **59**-17
가지 **113**-4
가지 **45**-9 **113**-4
가축 **115**
각막 **68**-12
각뿔 **120**-26
간 **69**-68
간식류 **48**-B
간이식당 **62**-18
간이식탁 **18**-32
간이 유모차 **20**-22
간이 침대 **17**-31
간장 **48**-32
간호사 **72**-2
갈기 **116**-32-a
갈다 **53**-4
갈매기 **118**-7
갈비 **47**-53
갈퀴 **29**-8
감기 **70**-8
감시대 **101**-2
감염 **70**-11
감자 **45**-25
감자 샐러드 **48**-12
감자껍질요리 **55**-6
감자칩 **48**-16
감자 튀김 **55**-21
감정 **42**
감청색 **56**-15
감탕나무 **113**-12
갓길 **94**-17
강 **114**-15
강낭콩 **45**-17
강당 **77**-13
강아지 **117**-54
강판 **19**-30
개 **50**-2 **50**-10 **51**-18 **117**-53
개구리 **119**-33
개똥벌레 **118**-34
개를 산책시키다 **9**-10
개미 **118**-45
개미핥기 **117**-48
개수대 **18**-5
개인 **98**-3
개인운동 **102**
개인 위생용품 **23**
객실 **97**-11
갤런 **51**-23 **52**
거리 **1**-7 **94** **94**-26 **120**-10
거리번호 **1**-6
거미 **118**-37
거미줄 **118**-37-a
거실 **14**
거울 **17**-18 **22**-18
거위 **118**-21
거친 **40**-40
거품기 **19**-31 **19**-39
걱정스러운 **43**-25
건강상태 **42**
건강차 **48**-41
건반악기 **112**-E
건의함 **90**-21
건전지 **29**-25
건초 **115**-9
건축기사 **80**-4
건포도 **44**-27
걷기 **102**-C
걷다 **108**-13
걸레 **24**-5
걸상 **10**-4
검사 **73**-14
검색 **96**
검안사 **72**-12
검정색 **56**-8
검정콩 **45**-16
겁먹은 **43**-26
게 **47**-68 **119**-16
게시판 **10**-23 **86**-4 **110**-34
게임 **109**-R
게임팩 **65**-35
겨드랑이 **68**-33
겨울 **98**-28
겨자 **48**-25
격자무늬의 **61**-19
견과류 **48**-22
견인차 **93**-92
결재서류함 **88**-5
결혼반지 **60**-3
경대 **17**-20
경련 **70**-22
경리부 **90**-26
경비원 **67**-16 **83**-19
경비하다 **84**-14
경적 **93**-60
경주용 자동차세트 **65**-18
경찰 **82**-10
경찰관 **39**-32
경찰서 **38**-2
곁들이 요리 **55**-D
계곡 **114**-5
계기판 **93**-48 **97**-4
계란 **46**-13
계량기 **49**-78
계량단위 **52**
계량스푼 **19**-18
계량컵 **19**-17
계산기 **10**-15 **64**-26 **87**-8
계산대 **49**-K **49**-74
계산원 **49**-80 **80**-14
계절 **98** **98**-C
계측 **120** **120**-A
고가도로 **94**-9
고객 **49**-73
고객 서비스 창구 **62**-17
고구마 **45**-26
고래 **119**-9
고릴라 **117**-47
고르덴 바지 **57**-11
고모 **3**-1
고모부 **3**-2
고무 스탬프 **88**-31
고무공 **65**-5
고무신 **59**-24
고무 젖꼭지 **21**-15
고무줄 **89**-7
고무풀 **89**-25
고삐 **102**-15
고속도로 **94** **94**-6
고슴도치 **116**-2
고양이 **117**-51
고양이에게 먹이를 주다 **9**-9
고용주 **86**-33
고전음악 **111**-1
고체풀 **89**-23
고추 **45**-29
고치 **118**-42-a
곡괭이 **91**-5
곤충 **118**
곤충류 **118**-B
곧은 **40**-17, 19
골무 **109**-6
골반 **68**-36
골절되다 **71**-46
골프 **102**-J
골프공 **102**-19
골프채 **102**-18
곰인형 **20**-1
곱슬곱슬한 **40**-20
곱하기 **31**
공구 **28**
공구상자 **28**-20
공구벨트 **91**-2
공기 매트리스 **101**-22
공기오염 **114**-24
공기펌프 **92**-40
공부하다 **9**-19
공사장 **91**
공사장 인부 **81**-17
공사장 현장감독 **81**-26 **90**-10
공상과학영화 **111**-23
공연 **110**
공예 **78**-17
공원 **36**-12 **100**
공작 **118**-27
공작세트 **65**-3
공장 **90**
공중전화 **39**-24
공중전화 박스 **39**-23
공책 **10**-11 **89**-12
공책지 **10**-12

어휘록

The **bold** number indicates the page(s) on which the word appears; the number that follows indicates the word's location in the illustration and in the word list on the page. For example, "north **5**-1" indicates that the word *north* is on page 5 and is item number 1.

주제별 색인